This practical, down-to-earth guide is ba
on four simple rules for efficient remembe
  1. Intend to remember; simply try.
  2. React actively to the experience you
     should remember.
  3. Refresh your memory of the experienc
     at strategic times.
  4. Keep your thoughts on the meanings
     of the experiences.

Dr. Donald A. Laird and Eleanor C. Laird are
the authors of "The Technique of Personal
Analysis," and other successful books on
selling and business practices.

McGRAW-HILL PAPERBACKS
PERSONAL AND PROFESSIONAL GUIDES

Prices subject to change without notice.

Techniques for Efficient Remembering

Donald A. Laird
Eleanor C. Laird

McGraw-Hill Book Company, Inc.
New York
Toronto
London

To the little girl who said,
"Memory is what I forget with"

Preface

The aim of this book is to build some bridges which will connect the ambitious general reader with the practical rather than the theoretical essence of thousands of research findings which bear on remembering and learning. James Clerk Maxwell's statement, "For the sake of persons of different types, scientific truth should be presented in different forms," gave us encouragement in this aim.

The only claim to originality is the attempt to boil down the essence of the findings into a few General Rules which provide guidance for self-improvement in remembering. These are called *general* because they can presumably be put to use to increase the efficiency of all sorts of remembering in general.

Only a few examples of how each General Rule can be applied are given. But since each rule emphasizes the "why" in addition to a little "how to," they should give the reader a basis for working out his own applications to more situations than it is possible to include in a small book. (One person who read the early manuscript commented: "This will be a 'how-to' book with a difference—a brave attempt to give the reader some understanding from which basis he can work out a 'memory system' which will meet his own individual needs.")

Although it is often difficult to differentiate between remembering and learning, the remembering aspects have been kept uppermost because of the practical person's greater interest in remembering.

The book also clings closely to those memories which can be intentionally recalled, and ignores the intriguing "subconscious memories" which are of more interest to the clinical psychologist than to the reader concerned with his personal efficiency. The so-called "diseases of memory" are also omitted.

The scientists mentioned are usually those who were the first to make the finding that is being presented. In most instances any one of a hundred experiments, some of them more clear-cut than the one cited, could have been used for illustrative purposes. But it seemed fitting to cite the name of the researcher who first broke new ground as a possible way to give each a merited measure of immortality.

Some portions of this book have appeared as articles, but in much different form, in *Today's Health, Trained Men,* and *Your Life* magazines.

> Donald A. Laird
> Eleanor C. Laird

Morainewood-on-Wabash

Contents

TECHNIQUES FOR EFFICIENT REMEMBERING

CHAPTER 1

The four General Rules

1. It's the workhorse for mental activity

Remembering is everybody's business, every minute. Luckily we can greatly increase—and easily—the amount and accuracy of what we remember. Simply apply a few principles which researchers have discovered.

Right at the start we should realize that remembering involves much more than recalling names or learning a poem by heart. Remembering cuts a much wider swath in our workaday lives. It is continuously required, for instance, in each of the 8 to 12 thoughts which Dr. David C. McClelland estimates pass through our heads every minute.

Remembering is a universal biological function which enables living creatures to steer their behavior so they can cope successfully with life. Remembering previous experiences— and especially their significance, or meaning—makes it pos-

1

sible to go through life with less trial-and-error blundering. There is less chance of getting burned twice if the inexhaustible miracle of memory is on the job.

Remembering enables us to bind the past to the present and future, and hence to modify our thoughts and actions on the basis of experience. *Time-binding* is what Count Alfred Korzybski called this aspect of remembering, and he made it one of the cornerstones of his system of general semantics, or science of meanings.

Remembering keeps the mental machinery active, and moving forward, by *circulating meaningful information* for it to work with. If there is little meaning remembered to circulate, there cannot be much worthwhile thinking to carry us forward. This is a cornerstone of cybernetics, which was originated by Dr. Norbert Wiener.

To illustrate the all-pervading role of remembering in daily life, here are lists of a very few of the situations in which it is essential. For each situation, the better we remember, the more efficiently the work or activity can be done. And we can't do any of them without remembering.

The role of remembering is obvious in:
Adding, subtracting, multiplying, dividing
Addresses recalled when wanted
Appointments remembered
Birthdays and other anniversaries kept in mind
Errands not overlooked
Instructions remembered
Names and faces under control
Reciting poetry, etc.
Sales points on tip of tongue
Telephone numbers recalled correctly
Less obvious, but remembering still essential in:
Decision-making
Finding way around

Keeping track of things
Learning any job, or anything else
Planning anything
Price and quality judgments
Reading anything
Social manners
Solving problems
Trouble shooting
Understanding what people say

Those lists could be extended to take in practically everything we do, including even worry and neurotic behavior. That may sound unreasonable, but just try making a list of things you can do in which remembering does not play a part in their doing. Such a nonmemory list would include only reflexes, such as sneezing, or physiological processes, such as digestion.

Remembering's greatest usefulness is probably as the workhorse for our mental activities—time-binding and circulating information. People have acquired amazing memory stunts, yet been so inefficient and idiotic they could not make a living—because the stunts did not help them bind time or circulate meaningful information.

2. Why Lonnie's wonderful memory was of little use

The story of Lonnie F., whom Dr. Martin Scheerer studied for several years, shows we should strive to use memory as a workhorse and not as a stunt.

Lonnie was a New Yorker with a tenacious remembrance for the names and birthdays of everyone he met. A year after a brief meeting he could quickly call out the name on sight, and as a bonus gleefully tell the person on what day of the week he had been born. Meeting people and learning their names and birthdays was his consuming interest.

Don't envy him yet. Except for that one-sided accomplishment, his thinking gave him scant help to cope with life. He did not know the difference between "short" and "long." He would conclude incorrectly that the taller of two persons was the older, although he remembered their birth years exactly. He was letter-perfect in repeating Lincoln's "Gettysburg Address," but didn't know what a president was.

Lonnie wouldn't have been much use around an office except to greet visitors—a job he would have loved. In fact, he could not get any job, despite his breath-taking memory stunts.

He had to be classified as feebleminded and was cared for by less spectacular people who used their remembering to build up meanings they could use in solving problems and planning their lives.

As for Lonnie's wonderful verbatim remembering, Dr. Scheerer and his colleagues concluded that any ordinary person could do as well as Lonnie. All that was required was that one should devote as much time and interest to it as Lonnie did.

But who wants to be a Lonnie? We should aim for something different.

3. *What to aim for*

As the story unfolds, it will become clear that most of us use our memory powers haphazardly. We scarcely begin to tap their full usefulness.

As an example, Dr. James H. Moore checked the amount the average person gets from his reading. He found that people usually recalled only slightly more than half of the distinct ideas they had read only a few moments previously —the world's greatest disappearing act.

That may not be as bad as it seems at first. After all, much idle-time reading has little value as a workhorse for thinking. But the troublesome fact is that people are almost as quick to forget important reading, such as job or safety instructions.

We don't want to aim at remembering everything. Some picking and choosing is necessary. We should give priority to two long-range objectives which are recognized as yielding the most useful returns from better remembering. We should use remembering:

To improve efficiency at work
As an aid to mental activity

This book is directed toward those two goals of better remembering.

There is wide room for improvement in reaching those goals, even by the best of us. Fortunately, there is now a substantial amount of soundly scientific information about how to go about making the improvement, as several hundred tests have proven beyond doubt. We will try to give you the essence of these discoveries, in a practical form which can be used for anything which you consider worth remembering.

4. The usefulness of "memory systems"

The ancient Greeks had schemes to help one remember odds and ends, but not to help the workhorse of mental activity. Some of those old systems, with only slight changes, are still in scattered use.

Some of these systems are of help in holding on to unrelated facts. Many teaching psychologists demonstrate a system to show students that it can be done. After demonstrating a system, however, the psychologists usually poohpooh it and point out that it has little usefulness except as a stunt. If the system is not an outright gold brick, it is at best

likely to be a detour which, for two reasons, produces lop-
sided remembering!

The systems use artificial systems which are not true to
life. And they fail to do the important things of binding-
time and circulating information—too much like Lonnie's
stunts to come to anything.

During Mark Twain's day these systems flourished and became fads for a time. The experts who traveled about the
country giving memory courses were generally odd char-
acters who could talk fluently and put on good shows. Sometimes they practiced hypnotism and sold herb medicines on
the side. Others had a sideline of phrenology and gave vo-
cational advice after "reading the skull." Still others added
to their incomes by conducting spiritualistic seances. Those
good old days must have been gullible days.

Theodore Dwight Weld, a character from Connecticut,
was one of the most picturesque of those memory experts,
both in appearance and conduct. His nose was twisted, and
one eye disfigured. A natural-born "soapboxer," he began his
public career as a revivalist, then made forays as a tem-
perance lecturer.

Weld himself could seldom remember the day of the week,
or what month it was. He had to look out a window to tell
whether it was summer or winter. He would hunt for his
spectacles while holding them in his hand. But those memory
lapses didn't keep him from setting up as a "professor of
memory training." He lectured so much that he lost his voice
for a time.

It was Weld, or another expert similar to him, who gave
Mark Twain the basis for his anecdote about the memory
lecturer who amazed his audience by remembering a hundred new names and faces, but walked out into the rain
after the lecture forgetting his umbrella and rubbers.

We are indebted to an entirely different variety of expert for our modern scientific knowledge about learning and remembering.

5. *Ebbinghaus laid the foundations*

The scientific study of remembering was started by a brilliant, plodding German, Herman Ebbinghaus, who became one of the first giants of experimental psychology. Ebbinghaus was only thirty-five in 1885 (the year after Weld died) when he published his first findings after twelve years of cautious experimentation. He was well-to-do, and financed his experiments himself; they were an epoch-making investment.

His little book *About Memory* created a stir in 1885. It is a classic, and remains on the market after all these years. (You can get a paperback copy from the University Store, Brown University, Providence, R.I.)

About the same year that Ebbinghaus started experimentation on memory several other things were hatching which were to become widely useful. Burroughs was bringing out his first adding machine, Felt his Comptometer, Mergenthaler his Linotype, Eastman his Kodak, Waterman the fountain pen, and Hollerith punch-card accounting. It was a great period—and Ebbinghaus was the only one of those mentioned who did not patent and strive to make a commercial venture of his work.

Following Ebbinghaus' scientific spadework, there have been several hundreds of careful experiments on every conceivable aspect of remembering, forgetting, and their close relative learning. On no other topic of psychology have there been as many useful and well-confirmed discoveries which make the old "systems" seem like one-horse shays in a jet age.

These discoveries point to the natural ways, as contrasted with artificial ways, for more efficient remembering and learning.

6. The General Rules to follow

An example is the way Dr. Fred S. Keller applied only a few of the principles to help soldiers memorize codes. His soldiers learned as well with only four hours of code practice a day as other soldiers did with seven hours' daily practice in which the rules were not followed.

There are several dozen workable principles which can make remembering more efficient. But that is too many to bear in mind. Accordingly, we have boiled these down to four General Rules (see following page) which are broad enough to include the essence of the larger number. This book is organized around these four General Rules which you can use for organizing your own remembering.

There is ample evidence that those four General Rules can double the efficiency of everyday remembering when they are followed. Many people who seem to have "naturally good memories" have been found to follow the principles, either intentionally or accidentally. And other people who complained about "a poor memory" have improved greatly— as the soldiers memorizing codes—when they deliberately applied the principles.

The four General Rules are worth applying intentionally until they become habits, because efficient remembering is essential if we are to make the most of whatever other talents we have.

A fifth Commonsense Rule needs to be added for very practical reasons, and we will take that up in the next chapter before turning to pointers about how to get the most benefits from the four General Rules.

GENERAL RULES *for* EFFICIENT REMEMBERING

I. Have a *mental set*, or intention, to remember accurately at the time; simply try to remember it.

II. *React actively* to the experience you should remember; look, listen, talk, think about it at the time it occurs.

III. *Refresh* your memory of it at *strategic times* to keep it accurate and from going stale.

IV. Keep your thoughts on the *meanings* of what you intentionally store away for binding-time and as a workhorse for your thinking.

(If you want to learn how to use the old-time memory systems, you need not pay from $10 to $100 for a course of lectures by a traveling wizard. You will find directions for most of the systems still being promoted in the books by Dr. Ian Hunter and Dr. Joyce Brothers which are listed in the recommended readings at the back of this book.)

CHAPTER 2

The fifth Commonsense Rule

1. FOLLOW VON HUMBOLDT'S EXAMPLE
2. USE REMINDER CALENDARS AND TICKLERS
3. WRITE DOWN NONROUTINE ACTIVITIES
4. NOTES TO MAKE FOR LONG-RANGE USE
5. USE THE REMINDERS TO HELP MEMORIZE
6. DON'T TRY TO SAVE PAPER

1. Follow Von Humboldt's example

We might as well face it before we go any further. Although the four General Rules will enable anyone to remember much better, we must admit the sad truth that no one can ever remember all he should.

Even the brainiest person forgets more than he remembers, and about half of what he believes he remembers is inaccurate. In view of these natural limitations, it behooves us to form special habits of working efficiency which will spare us the risk of foolishly trying to carry everything in our heads.

That is why we need a fifth and supremely practical rule: *Write it down.*

The surest, quickest, and easiest way to remember better is to follow a reminder system and write down the things

10

that should be written down. About the biggest step toward improving working efficiency is to start this practice on a firm basis. After that, make use of the four General Rules.

In this chapter we will outline what, when, and how to make and organize reminders. In later chapters we will give additional details about getting the most out of this Commonsense Rule.

Most of the world's achievers have made steady use of this rule. They have always carried memo books or batches of file cards to use to store the facts away in fadeproof black-and-white.

The fabulous Baron Alexander von Humboldt, the most productive scientist of his time, was an example. Lesser people imagined they could remember without writing it down, which doubtless helped keep them lesser people.

This was amusingly illustrated while Von Humboldt was exploring Mexico and making the first accurate map of that land. The native who guided him through the countryside around Mexico City did not see why the baron was considered a genius. The guide admitted the baron was a quick-moving hard worker. "The baron couldn't have a good memory," the guide said with a contemptuous shrug, "because he had to write down the names of villages and streams which everyone knew."

But the brilliant baron knew, as you should, that things slip from even the best memory. The safest way to hold on to what you will need to use later, and to be sure it is correct when you do use it, is to

1. Write it down systematically
2. Organize the jottings consistently

This Commonsense Rule is especially needed as one advances in responsibility and has more irons in the fire. It is the only way to get around the ceilings on the memory span, or on how much one can keep in mind at one time. These ceilings are rather low, and most high-level jobs require remembering more than the memory span can hold on to unaided.

Writing it down also becomes more essential as one becomes older. After a ten-year research on aging and human skill, Dr. A. T. Welford advised workers and executives who are past fifty: "Write it down; don't try to keep it in your head."

A few people hesitate to make notes because they are overconfident, or too busy, or too lethargic to take the time to write it down for future consultation.

Others neglect it deliberately, because of two false beliefs. One is that writing it down would be an admission of weakness. The other is the supposition that they will develop more memory power if they depend upon memory alone, which is nonsense, as the next chapter will show.

So these folks try to jam their heads with more minor details than any memory span can manage. They inevitably get fouled up by forgetting appointments, errands, instructions, conversations, and anything else that can slip the mind —and anything can, as the millions of unclaimed bank deposits illustrate.

Chores are more likely to be taken care of when they are in writing and staring us in the face. Seasoned executives who follow this Commonsense Rule (and most of them do) also use strategies to make sure the other person has a forget-proof written reminder to stare at him.

Thus the executive sends the other person a note summarizing, say, the agreements reached in their conversation. Or he uses telegrams, rather than telephone calls, even within his own city, because the telegram will be right there to keep reminding the other person.

Another application of this has been emphasized by the New York State Health Department. "When you hire a baby-sitter, don't trust her memory," they advise. Give her a written sheet of instructions.

What should be written down for one's own use? Not everything, of course. Some guides are needed to help one decide whether to make a note or to take a chance on re-membering it. The most dangerous guide is a feeling that it will surely be remembered so doesn't need to be put in black-and-white.

There are four classes of material, or chores, which can usually be handled with greatest efficiency with a suitable note system. For the balance of this chapter we will give only a quick outline of these.

2. *Use reminder calendars and ticklers*

Business in which *future dates* are involved should always be written on a calendar, or in a tickler file arranged by dates. In addition to keeping the current week, or month, in front of you, thumb ahead to get advance warnings of what is coming up. Examples:

> Appointments made (with outline of points to consider)
> Appointments to be made in the future (dental, eye, medical examinations, flu shots, etc.)
> Birth dates and anniversaries
> Calls to make (with outline of points to take up)
> Coming events of interest
> Contract dates
> Dates to follow up propositions
> Deadlines (with a warning an ample time ahead)
> License renewal dates

    Meetings coming up
    Payments due
    Promises you have made
    Reports due
    Reviews of investments, insurance, etc.

Write the date down the instant you learn about it. It is reckless to assume that you will remember to write it down later. If you are away from the calendar when a date is set, write it on a file card at once, and transfer it to the calendar the first thing when you get back to your desk.

3. Write down nonroutine activities

Special chores, or close-at-hand nonroutine business, should also be written down to jog the memory and stare at you until the business is disposed of.

Notes for these can be made on a pocket pad or file card, and the note can usually be tossed away when the mission is accomplished. In addition to reminding one of the chore, these notes are useful for organizing the day's work in an efficient sequence, such as making telephone calls in a batch, or to save steps in routing outside visits. Examples:

    Errands
    Information you want to get
    Letters to write (with points to include)
    Messages to deliver
    Phone calls to make (with outline of points)
    Questions for discussion
    Shopping list
    Whom you want to talk with today (and about what)

You can't get things done when you forget to do them. The self-memos of this variety will keep nonroutine details in front of you and prod you to get on with them. Thus more can be accomplished, and without danger of overreaching your memory span.

4. Notes to make for long-range use

There are other things which should be written down and *filed away* more or less permanently. These are matters which will likely be useful in the future when they may have become dim in memory, but when you should have the facts without error or omission. In general, these items relate to one's career rather than to day-by-day details, and are commonly neglected. Examples:

> Agreements, conferences; some of these notes should be read and initialed by other participants
> Anything about which you may have to testify later
> Employment record, including dates, duties, salary, names of chiefs
> Dental record
> Ideas dealing with inventions or discoveries; for legal reasons these should be dated and also signed by a witness
> Medical records which may provide lifesaving information
> Speeches you have made
> Tax records

Some of the notes in this classification may turn out to be so valuable in the future that they might well be stored in a fire-resistant cabinet, or safe, along with investment and insurance records.

5. Use the reminders to help memorize

The written reminder does more than serve as a substitute for remembering. Details are actually registered a little better as a result of giving some attention to writing them down. Moreover, the jottings can be used to guide you in reviewing so you will have fuller and more accurate retention; we will

take up later the efficient use of the notes for brushing up.
Examples:

> Formulas
> Information of career value
> Names (with description of faces)
> Prices, rates
> Reading of career significance
> Specifications
> Words and meanings (foreign, technical, English)

The written reminders for these should be (a) carried
with you and reviewed from time to time until they seem
to be remembered, and (b) then filed away systematically
so they can readily be consulted in the future.

6. Don't try to save paper

There is an art to making notes so they will be serviceable
reminders. As a fluttery housewife learned when, in a burst of
pseudo-efficiency she wrote down her appointments:

> 2:30 Thursday
> 9:30 Friday

But she neglected to write down which Thursday, and also
which was with the dentist and which with the beauty
parlor.

Or the mechanic who put a card on his machine in order
to keep a record of when he oiled it. When he did oil it he
simply made a check mark on the card, and did not write the
date of oiling.

The common weakness is to make the reminders too
skimpy, perhaps to save time. But a too-brief note can waste
time. You made a note to phone Mr. Tinsley, but wrote it
briefly: "Call T." That afternoon you were not sure whether

the "T" stood for Thomas, Timmons, Tankersly, or which Mr. T—or what it was you wanted to talk over with him.

Make the reminder complete enough so it will be clear to you a year later. If you are in doubt whether it is complete enough, that doubt usually indicates that you need to write a little more detail. A good guide, especially for long-range reminders, is to have them well labeled and so complete that your successor could follow through if you were struck dead tomorrow.

> If you want to get things done that depend on remembering, write them down and keep them where they keep looking you in the face.

Now we are ready to take up some things which may surprise you about how memory operates. But these will be instructive surprises.

CHAPTER 3

Remembering numbers illustrates some fundamentals

1. Practice remembering helps only a little

Everybody has to remember numbers, but many everyday numbers are so long they overtax the normal memory span. Remembering numbers, accordingly, can be used to illustrate some basic facts about the best ways to go about remembering.

Children starting school have a memory span for five numerals, on the average. They can call back correctly a string of five numbers immediately after hearing them once. The span becomes a bit longer as they grow older.

Dr. Arthur I. Gates had beginning school children practice memorizing numerals for three months. This steady practice increased their memory span for numbers. That seemed encouraging.

But two other findings showed him that the practice had been mostly a waste of time. (1) The steady practice with numbers did not increase the children's remembering of other things. (2) After the summer vacation, with practice discontinued, they backslid so that their span for numbers was no better than it would have been without any practice. The long practice with numbers did not permanently strengthen their memories even for numbers.

Those findings have been abundantly confirmed by many experimenters, using all sorts of memory material. So we have to give up our worship of the merits of mere practice and resign ourselves to these facts:

Mere practice helps remembering only as long as we keep on practicing

It usually helps us remember only the material practiced on, and does not help us remember other things

Something different from mere practice is needed to improve the efficiency of remembering. As we turn to some other ways to improve memory, there will be some instructive surprises in store.

2. A little stretching helps more

Many vocations deal with numbers from morning until the closing chime. Workers in these types of jobs run into trouble if they have to work beyond their memory span for numbers.

Although the average adult can handle a span of eight numerals, there are individual differences. (Women are, in general, no better than men in memory span for numbers, though women commonly excel men in remembering words.) A few adults can remember a span of ten successfully; Dr. Alfred Binet studied a "lightning calculator" who could remember the astonishing span of forty-two numerals. A few adults, on the other hand, are sunk when it comes to numbers, and are at their limit with a span of only four numerals —and the difficulty they have remembering telephone numbers!

His Scotland Yard bodyguard for twenty years reports that Sir Winston Churchill had difficulty with numbers. He was also forever forgetting his reading glasses, and occasionally his false teeth. Despite those weak spots in his remembering, Sir Winston was a wizard at remembering meanings.

Many business executives find it easy to remember numbers, and keep a wide range of business figures tenaciously in mind. This is a real help in guiding their decisions if they also associate the practical meaning or significance of the numbers.

Because of such individual differences, many firms test a prospective employee for his number span before placing him in work where he would have to keep numbers in mind. (Our book *Sizing Up People* is devoted entirely to such individual differences in abilities and capacities.)

Some firms have redesigned their numbering systems, along lines we will summarize shortly, so numbers are easier to remember. This is a variety of job simplification which enables more people to master the work.

It is possible, however, for a person to stretch himself once in a while and handle slightly longer numbers than his usual span. Thus the man with a natural span of seven can remember a span of eight or even nine by making a special effort. This stretching combines General Rule I (Try to remember) and General Rule II (React actively and fully).

But there is a limit to stretching. When you stretch too much, something gives. If a man with a natural span of seven tries to handle a span of ten, his memory usually shrinks down to five or six.

Go ahead and stretch yourself a little, but not too much. Stretch yourself often.

3. Grouping helps still more

Grouping is one of the simplest ways to organize remembering along the lines nature rewards. This was shown by tests Drs. Pauline Martin and Samuel Fernberger made when they put young men to work memorizing long numbers over a four-month period.

The men could hold on to a span of eight numerals at the start. Once in a while they could stretch themselves and retain a span of ten. They failed, at first, on lists of twelve numerals.

Then something happened. One of the men remembered a span of twelve numerals which the experimenters had read to him at a uniform pace.

How come? The man had hit upon the idea of grouping the long series into batches of three as he heard them, like this:

$$493 \quad 295 \quad 638 \quad 572$$

By grouping them mentally that way, he had to remember only three at a time.

The longest grouping of that sort the men could handle was in fives. When one thought he could include six in a group, it set him back—overstretching.

But by reasonable stretching, and by grouping, it became possible for the men to remember a span of fourteen numerals—close to doubling their spans.

Any permanent improvement in their remembering came, not from practice as such, but from having discovered the secret of grouping.

4. How to use grouping

Grouping is a permanently useful aid because it breaks things too long to remember into smaller bites which are easy to retain and recall. That is one reason we have grouped the numerous principles for efficient remembering into the four General Rules, plus the fifth Commonsense Rule.

If you want to remember a long telephone number, use the principle of grouping. Take the number 3–2264. The telephone company has already done some grouping for you, by putting a dash in the number. They call this a "dent," and it is used deliberately to make the number easier to keep in mind.

You may also have noticed that professional operators put in an additional dent when they speak the number. They give slight emphasis to every other numeral after the dash, like this:

$$3\text{--}22 \ 64$$

Thus the longer number is heard as a series of two-place numbers which are easy to remember. The rhythm in the sound may also help remembering.

The Social Security numbering system—167–18–1051—is another illustration of how grouping makes it easier (but still a job!) to remember king-size numbers.

When numbers have to be longer than the usual memory span, a letter inserted in the grouping helps. Dr. Clarence W. Young found that this little change was effective in increasing the span remembered.

Some firms combine numbers and letters not only to make remembering more efficient, but also to give essential information. This brings in General Rule IV (Meanings). This amounts to a secret code, which is a great assist to those who are in on the secret. Here is an example:

```
  37  P  7405  N
  37  means  paint
   P  means  stored in corridor P
7000  means  enamel
 400  means  quick-drying
   5  means  light blue color
   N  means  no discounts on less than carload lots
```

Grouping is also used in mail-order catalogs, and in department-store advertising. And in window displays.

Reports are likely to be better grasped and remembered when the topics are grouped in four or five sections. Each section deals with one aspect, or meaning (General Rule IV).

That speech, or sermon, you remembered was probably grouped around a few points which fitted together naturally.

As an accountant expressed it, grouping improves the break-even point.

Whenever you have long lists to remember:

Group them into smaller units
Group them into assortments which go naturally together

5. Most gained when several rules are applied

What happens when a beginner in memory improvement tries to use several guides? One of the first tests of that was made by Dr. Herbert Woodrow. He gave young adults, all high-school graduates, brief explanations of the following natural principles which help one remember:

Use grouping and rhythm
Be confident you can remember it
Visualize—see it in your mind's eye
Try to remember and to recall it
Memorize by meanings rather than by sounds
Try to remember the whole thing, not a bit at a time

Keep what you want to remember in the center of your
attention

Associate it with things you already remember

After the people were enlightened about how to use those
principles, they were given tests on remembering poetry,
prose, miscellaneous facts, historical dates, numbers, words.
They remembered 36 per cent better than they had on
similar tests before they knew about using those principles.
Vastly better than mere practice could have accomplished.

Are such gains likely to last? One of the first to check on
that question was Dr. Sidney L. Pressey, who taught a few
of the principles to college students who were on the brink
of flunking their courses. Their grades began to improve
right away. In addition, they were still doing better a year
afterward. We can be pretty sure that they remembered
better all their lives—provided they kept on applying the
principles.

> The only practice that will improve your remembering is
> practice in applying rules based on the natural laws of
> remembering.

6. "Good-by memory ... welcome remembering!"

Why doesn't exercise strengthen memory? It strengthens
muscles.

The modern answer may knock your ideas of memory
endwise. This is the story.

Centuries ago the word *memory* came into use for an imaginary place where memories were stored. Because there is a
word for it, people took it for granted that there was "a
memory."

But you will not find a modern scientist who believes that
we have "a memory." Such a thing as "a memory" is now

considered as much a myth as the notion that the moon is made of green cheese.

What we do have is the capacity to retain and later to recall some of our past experiences. Remembering is something we do, not a substance or anything tangible that resides in some part of the head. It is a function—a series of processes—which is vitally useful for making the most of our other talents and functions. And we can follow principles to improve in our use of the processes involved in this function, although we cannot strengthen a nonexistent memory by exercising it.

Remembering, then, is not a fixed quantity, or some substance, or a location inside the head. It is a series of processes which can function better than it has in the past if we direct it properly.

That is why this is a book on remembering, not on memory.

But as our language has developed, memory is a handy word to use. Whenever it is used in this book—and we hope in your thinking—it does not refer to A Memory, but to some aspect of the processes of remembering.

So we say "Good-by memory, welcome remembering!" as we turn to get a working acquaintance with the natural principles which we can apply so remembering will function at its best for anything we think worth remembering. The next two chapters will deal with motivation for remembering.

RULE I

Have a mental set, or intention, to remember accurately at the time—simply try to remember

---

CHAPTERS:

CHAPTER 4

Have a mental set to remember

1. REMEMBERING DOESN'T JUST HAPPEN
2. YOU'LL REMEMBER MORE IF YOU TRY TO
3. APPLICATIONS OF TRYING TO REMEMBER
4. SELF-DIRECTION BETTER THAN CONCENTRATION
5. MAKE YOUR TRY AT THE START OF THE CYCLE

1. Remembering doesn't just happen

The letter Richard H. was dictating was short, but he had to ask in a hesitant voice, "Read back the first paragraph— I've forgotten how I started out."

Eunice H. attended church regularly, and with her head bowed had listened reverently to the same benediction hundreds of times. She felt like a hardened sinner when she was asked to repeat the benediction and found that she did not remember it.

Slender Evelyn G. posted accounts all day. One afternoon the supervisor asked if she had yet posted the Murphy Company account, and Evelyn couldn't remember. A look at the ledger cards showed, however, that she had posted it about fifteen minutes before.

Thirtyish Pauline R. worked in a small loan office which was held up while she was alone at lunch hour. Twenty minutes after the robbery, when the police asked her to describe the robber, all she could remember was that it was a man. A detective looked at the ceiling and muttered, "Isn't that just like a woman!"

Those instances, as do most instances of poor remembering, illustrate the most common cause: people simply assume they will remember, and they do not try to remember at the time a thing happens.

We certainly can't count on remembering just happening of its own accord. When there is something we should remember, we have to turn on our remembering machinery. Poor remembering has been figuratively called a deficiency disease because it is so often due to insufficient effort to remember things at the time they take place.

That is why remembering remains one of our most underused capacities.

> Don't expect remembering to happen without any help from you; help it happen.

2. You'll remember more if you try to

Our memory is caught off balance when things occur unless we are set to remember them.

A demonstration made by Dr. James H. Moore is one of many which shows the great usefulness of merely trying to remember. He asked a group of people to count the words in a little story. They gave careful attention to each word, but afterward could recall on the average only seven of the ideas they had seen in the story. They did not have a mental set of trying to remember what they read.

Then another group was asked to read the same story, and to try to remember as much of it as possible. They recalled

fifty-one of the ideas in the story—seven times more remembered as a result of simply trying to. (And did you recognize Dr. Moore's name, which was given in Chapter 1?
Or did you read that chapter without a mental set of trying
to remember?)

The closest thing yet discovered to a pushbutton for remembering is the simple effort to try to remember.

How long we retain it, as well as how much we hold on to,
is also determined to a large degree by the mental set at
the time we are getting the original impressions. Dr. Albert
Aall was the first to demonstrate this in the laboratory.

Ignace Paderewski, whose red hair was bright enough to
light a candle, learned that lesson firsthand before he became
a world-famous pianist. While still a struggling would-be
artist, he crammed for two weeks to memorize a dozen
selections for a recital. Three days after the recital he could
not play any of the selections from memory. That shocked
him into thenceforth memorizing selections with the intention of remembering them for a long time.

Dr. Foster P. Boswell tested this problem with students
who were memorizing Chinese words. When checked two
weeks later, they remembered 6 per cent more when they
had memorized with permanent retention in view.

We can now understand why students who cram for an
examination can't recall much of their cramming the day
after the examination. That is why a goodly share of education goes down the drain.

> If you want it to linger longer in memory, memorize it with
> the deep intention of retaining it a long while.

3. Applications of trying to remember

Do you think you could shuffle a deck of cards, study
their arrangement for twenty minutes, and then close your

eyes and recall the order in which the fifty-two had been shuffled? Wait a minute before answering.

Dr. Carl I. Hovland reported about a traveling entertainer who used that stunt to amaze college students. They did not think it humanly possible to do, but could not detect any trickery. So they asked a university psychologist if the "memory expert" was a fraud or a genius.

"Have you tried it yourselves?" he countered. They hadn't, but at his suggestion started to try. Shortly their amazement shifted direction.

One student could remember the order of all fifty-two freshly shuffled cards after his first twenty-minute study of them. Twelve students did it the third time they tried. The average did it after five or six warming-up tries. Those who succeeded soonest had hit upon the principle of grouping the cards, as was described in the preceding chapter.

A practical application of trying to remember was made in a chemical plant where dangerous materials were handled. New workers were always given a printed list of safety regulations to study before they went to work. But foremen complained that the new workers were turning them prematurely gray by ignoring the safety rules.

A check showed that the new workers were not ignoring the rules intentionally. They simply did not remember them from reading them in their usual reading manner. The trouble disappeared after the newcomers were instructed to read the vital rules with the firm resolve to remember them.

In training retail salespeople it has also been found necessary to emphasize that they should try to remember the details of what the customer requests. So that when a dress with a V neck is asked for they don't start showing one with a square neck. It is more than listening politely to the customer; it requires the mental set of trying to remember the details for as long as the sale is under way.

"I forgot" is likely to mean "I didn't try to remember."

4. Self-direction better than concentration

Our mental processes usually function as we direct them to at the time. This determining tendency, as it is called, is more powerful than old-fashioned concentration and is worth knowing about and using.

When we direct our thoughts to posting accounts accurately, we don't remember much about the names and amounts. In order to remember any details of the account, we would need a mental set to remember the details; we would need to be in the mood to remember, which would doubtless slow down the work.

When we have a determining tendency to say something clever when introduced to people, we shouldn't wonder why we can't remember their names. If you want to remember the names, you should have a mental set to remember them when you first hear them, not to make a brilliant remark.

As a close-at-hand example, the subheadings throughout this book have been planned to arouse determining tendencies which will lead you to note one thing rather than another.

With the proper determining tendency, or mental set, no one needs to screw himself into a tense posture to concentrate on what he wants to remember.

The people who counted the words in the story for Dr. Moore screwed themselves up to get the words in sharper attention than the other group did, but they had little determining tendency to remember the story.

The young men who memorized the deck of freshly shuffled cards had a strong determining tendency to do the stunt themselves. That determining tendency took care of the concentrating for them.

When you have a determining tendency which touches off an earnest try to remember something, then concentration will come naturally as you tackle it. You will not have to bite lips, strain eyes, or seek refuge in a soundproof room to concentrate on it.

The intention—or motivation—to remember makes concentrating almost automatic. But it seldom works the other way around. You can concentrate until your eyes ache yet not remember, unless you have a confident mental set of trying to remember it, and to remember it for a long time, if that is what you want. That is why the following chapter deals with getting the motivation that makes one try to remember.

5. *Make your try at the start of the cycle*

"But I am trying hard to remember," the loan-office clerk shrieked back at the police as they asked her to try hard to recall the appearance of the robber.

She was making the try too late in the cycle. A try to remember will not help much unless it is made at the right time.

What we call remembering is actually a cycle which has four stages or phases, which were first described by Dr. Robert S. Woodworth. These stages are so distinct that it is scarcely an exaggeration to say that remembering is at least four things, or four processes.

These phases occur one after the other, in a well-established sequence to make a memory complete. Some memory aids are helpful in one part of the cycle, but not in other parts.

The stages, or the *Four R's of Remembering*, and the order in which they normally take place, are:

    1st. *Register* the experience (reading, hold up, name, instructions, or what not) so it makes an impression, or trace, in the nervous system.

    2nd. *Retain* the trace of it for a longer or shorter time.

    3rd. *Recall* the experience by rearousing the appropriate traces at some future time when it is wanted.

    4th. *Recognize* the recalled experience as a previous happening which has meaning for you.

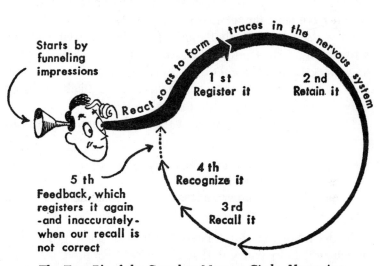

The Four R's of the Complete Memory Circle. *Narrowing lines* indicate weak regions in the circle. The traces may last for years, but are steadily being erased. *Distance between arrows* shows that some phases are shorter than others. The duration of a phase varies from one memory to another.

When the police questioned the jittery clerk about the holdup she tried to get answers at the stage of recall. But at that part of the cycle trying is not of much use. In fact, it generally helps most at this stage if one does not try too hard, as we will take up in Chapters 15 and 16.

Trying to remember is exceedingly helpful, however, at the first stage.

We should make the try to remember at the time things are happening—difficult to do, perhaps, in the excitement of a holdup, but entirely possible if one has been trained to keep cool by trying to remember. Intending to remember after the excitement is over is likely to be a waste of good intentions, and has led witnesses to recall imaginary details which have sent innocent men to prison.

So we see by now that most of us do our trying at the wrong time. The trying is neglected until we are stumped as we try to recall something that has slipped from mind. And at that phase of the cycle a hard try is likely to bring only false recognizing as its reward.

Do your trying at the start of the cycle, when impressions are being registered.

> Never take it for granted that you will remember, because you probably will not.
>
> Intend to remember, instead, when something is worth retaining.

In the following chapter we will look at some guideposts which will help you get that intention to remember what you judge worth remembering by being motivated to remember efficiently.

CHAPTER 5

How to build motives which make remembering purposive

1. Memory needs managing

We shouldn't complain about forgetting—actually we remember vast amounts. The trouble is more likely to be that we remember inconsequential things that are of no use later in coping with life. This was the case with Lonnie.

It is a kindly provision of Nature to let us tuck away only a tiny share of our experiences and thoughts. Imagine how overstuffed and confused our heads would be if we could recall every one of the estimated 10,000 thoughts we have during a day. How long-winded and scatter-brained we might be!

Because we usually let memory do as it pleases, we have a crazy-quilt patchwork of memories of this and that. Of odds and ends which sometimes make little sense. Of bits and pieces that are not of much use when we have to solve some problem. The scraps that are stored away at random make people impractical, inefficient, and muddleheaded.

What is almost always needed is not a "stronger memory," but better management of the one we have.

2. Goals help manage memory

Motives give a purpose for remembering.

Purposive remembering means that the person has some strong motives which lead him to remember certain things rather than other things. An amusing example was Jedediah Buxton, a native of old England, who could neither read nor write. He was overpowered, however, by the motive to remember every free drink that had been given him in the alehouse since he was twelve years old. (A memory stunt which, of course, won him many free mugs of ale, which may have been a part of his motive.)

An essential step toward purposive remembering is to have some personal goals which give one the foresight to try to remember things which bear on reaching these goals.

The goals need not deal directly with remembering, such as "I will learn Spanish." The most effective goals will likely be those life aims which focus on the results to be reached by better remembering.

For example, a goal of "I want to work my way into the export department" may stimulate most progress toward mastering Spanish. Such a career or achievement goal gives one an intention to pick up and retain whatever is run across that bears on reaching the goal. Motivation to remember is sharpened when we set up the right goals.

Some techniques have been found to be better than others for giving goals that produce results. Four of these are important enough that we will look into each of them.

3. Set your goals yourself

The goals we set for ourselves usually have the most influence on our remembering. This is one place where do-it-yourself is assuredly the best way. (There is much more about self-set goals in our book *The New Psychology for Leadership*.)

This helps us understand why all the compulsory years spent in school do not produce the learning they might. The board of education sets the goals, and teachers have an uphill job trying to transplant the goals into the pupils. The pupils wander through their prescribed studies with sparse results, because they have no self-determined goals to give a purpose for remembering the subjects.

It is different with those who go on to technical or business schools. Those students then have a purpose, or achievement motive, which is usually of their own making. It is a safe bet that those who take the technical courses because of their own purpose remember much more of the subjects than do those who are going through the motions to satisfy the family or company. Those who are working their way through, for instance, usually get the most for their money.

Many adults, like most grade-school pupils, have no goals which give them purposes for remembering. Their achievement motives are weak, or missing.

And if a supervisor, or job trainer, tries to set goals for them, the goals are not usually accepted wholeheartedly by the employees, and as a result not only job performance but also job learning (remembering) lags.

What to do about such weak motivation? Two things to start with.

Set some goals for yourself.
Guide or lead others to set goals for themselves instead of imposing ready-made goals on them.

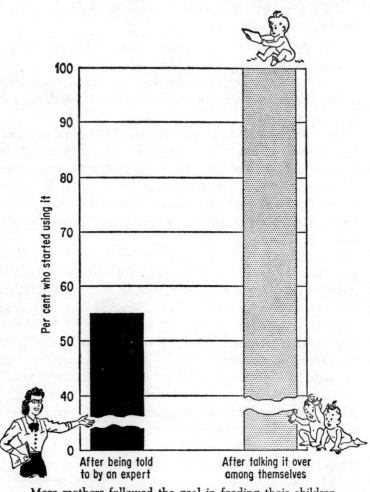

More mothers followed the goal in feeding their children when they set the goal themselves. (The goal was the same for both groups.) (Data from Dr. Marion Radke-Yarrow)

4. Make your goals definite and clear

The goals we set should be definite if they are to give most purpose to our remembering.

"I'm going to try to remember better" is a common resolve humans are forever making. But it is too vague—it covers everything, pins down nothing—to be of much help toward managing memory.

Such a vague goal may motivate a person to exert himself, but it does not give him targets to aim at. About the best it does is to stimulate him to be an eager beaver who hops-skips-and-jumps in all directions. If it helps remembering at all, it is likely to lead him to accumulate more odds and ends until he is stuffed with useless information.

The goal should be definite enough to give clear guidance as to what to pick and choose to remember. For example:

"I'm going to prepare for the diesel business" is more definite than "I'm going to have some sort of business of my own."

"I'm going to study up on petroleum stocks" is more definite and will help remembering more than "I'm going to make money as fast as I can."

> Set goals which are definite enough to give you a mental set for retaining definite things.

5. Set goals you can reach promptly

Close-at-hand goals which can be reached within the near future help remembering more than do faraway goals which cannot be reached until the distant future, if at all. Also, close-at-hand goals are less likely to cause discouragement.

If there is a chance to get into the export department within two months, that study of Spanish will progress much faster than if it might not be needed until some far-off or indefinite date.

"I am going to do a section on accounting each night" is more effective than "I want to finish an accounting course sometime."

"I am going to learn two new words a day" sets a closer goal than "I am going to improve my command of language when I get a chance." It also gives a basis for keeping tabs on your progress, which is always helpful in self-management.

Long-range, faraway goals are desirable, of course. But each should be broken down into sub-goals which will make day-by-day remembering more in line with the ultimate purpose. The two examples—a section of accounting, and two words a day—illustrate how long-range goals can be broken into close-at-hand goals.

> Set some goals which will give an immediate purpose for remembering various things.

6. Set goals which keep going on

On-going goals keep remembering purposive, day after day. In contrast, remembering is likely to slump if it is motivated by self-limiting goals. We will learn more about this when we take up the Zeigarnik effect in a later chapter.

A deadline is an example of a self-limiting, or terminal, goal. It stimulates a spurt of effort until the deadline is reached. Then comes the letdown, and remembering falls back to the usual haphazard basis. The striving to remember ends.

Cramming for an examination is an example of a self-limiting goal. As soon as the examination is taken, the purpose for remembering is gone. In addition, as we have already seen, a large share of what was remembered on examination day quickly fades beyond recall.

On-going goals are much different in their results. They give us a persistent purpose, not one-shot motives.

On-going goals also let us keep tabs on progress. There is a daily record of something more remembered. Although the achievement on one day—two new words—may not be earth-shaking, it does give the encouraging feeling that one is getting somewhere with remembering the things one wants to remember.

Set on-going goals which will give you
    (a) a persistent purpose, and
    (b) a running check on your progress toward the long-range goals you have set for yourself.

7. *Applied when moving to a new neighborhood*

The Census Bureau reports that one fifth of the people in the United States move each year. Each move requires a lot of fresh remembering. So many new things have to be caught on to that the memory span is stretched to the point of diminishing returns the first few weeks.

"So help me, I'll never move again," many say during this confusing period—only to forget the trials and embarrassments and move again within about five years to another place where they hope the grass will be greener.

Slowness about remembering the many details of the new location is a factor which makes some people homesick. Until they begin to get used to the new neighborhood, to remember the names and faces, the new place seems strange and prisonlike.

Any homesickness, in turn, quite likely makes it more difficult for one to catch on to the new details. The homesick brooding prevents the making of an adequate reaction to the new surroundings, which consequently slip from mind, or perhaps never get into the mind to begin with (General Rule II).

It is estimated that it takes at least six weeks for a person to get used to a new location, when he goes about remembering in the usual unintentional fashion and neglects to use purposive remembering.

Some suburban communities try to help the new family get acquainted by putting on a neighborhood party. Companies, military stations, and colleges usually have similar welcome parties for those who have moved in.

Those mass introductions, however, leave much to be desired. The spirit of welcome does help the greenhorn feel accepted, but there are too many names and faces for any human memory to get straight in an hour. A wonderful time may be had by all, but the face the newcomer recalls is a tantalizing blurred composite, and the name remembered is another embarrassing composite of babble-babble.

The newcomer will get the hang of names and faces better if he sets goals that are in step with the four techniques we have just outlined, like this:

The techniques	*The goals*
(a) Set it yourself.	(a) "I will actively try ...
(b) Make it specific, clear.	(b) to learn the names and faces of three neighbors ...
(c) Close-at-hand.	(c) each day ...
(d) On-going to completion.	(d) until I can easily recall and recognize each."

Goals like those, earnestly followed, will help remembering much more than would a burning but vague desire to be more popular in the new locality than in the one left behind.

Similar goals can be set up for the other remembering problems that beset a newcomer—such as finding the way to shopping centers, around the downtown stores, the library and parks, one-way streets and no-left-turns. A similar procedure should be used for getting a working acquaintance with local news and civic activities.

The magic in such goals is that they make one remember more of the useful things. Simply have intentional purposes, crystallized into goals for remembering something—anything, even free drinks, if you wish. That purpose automatically primes you to try to remember whatever bears on the goal at the time it occurs—you make the try at the part of the memory cycle where a try produces results (Chapter 4).

You'll feel more at home in the new locality, and sooner, with purposive remembering.

8. Applied when starting a new job

The typical worker changes to a new job every three to four years.

Remembering looms up as a problem when each new job is started. This may be more acute for the young person going to work for the first time, but it can also tangle up the experienced worker who is changing employers.

As with moving to a new locality, it probably takes at least six weeks before a person gets his bearings on a new job with a small firm. Some of the larger corporations estimate that it takes five years for a person to remember the ins and outs around the firm.

During the initial period of bewilderment on a new job, a small share of workers give up and quit in confusion before they know the lay of the land. Employers expect the new worker to be a costly producer until he is broken in for the particular firm and his new surroundings.

Company officials usually go out of their way to point out

what should be remembered; naturally, they want to keep breaking-in costs low. But fellow workers may do the opposite and point out nothing. Or do worse and point out the wrong things.

White-collar workers, as a rule, extend a helping hand to the new man. Some of them, however, look upon the new man as a future competitor who might displace them. To keep an upper hand in the competition, these apprehensive old-timers are secretive about essential job details and give little assistance in showing new workers what they would be wise to remember.

The blue-collar workers are the ones who are most likely to throw roadblocks in the way of the new man catching on to the job. This is especially so when the newcomer is one the employees think should be "trimmed down to size." Or when they size him up as an eager beaver who may be so conscientious about producing that he will be a record-breaker.

A good share of blue-collar workers are inclined to give any newcomer, whether he deserves it or not, some hazing before accepting him as one of the crew. Although usually done in the spirit of innocent merriment, these jokes and roadblocks do not help the new man remember the essential details—somewhat like learning how to make additions incorrectly for the fun of it.

When an older worker, or job trainer, is delegated to coach the new worker, as is done in some firms, the coach points out what are roadblocks and what should be remembered as part of the job. We can make a guess that half of new workers are put to work, however, without much more guidance than showing them how to find the rest room.

In case no coach is provided, the new worker has to guide himself, and there are several aids he can use in doing this:

• Take for granted that everything the supervisor or lead man tells you is worth remembering. Try to remember it.

• Assume that the names of tools, materials, operations, and parts are worth remembering. Try to remember them.

• The safety rules merit priority. Try to remember them.

• New words heard in connection with the work should be listened for. Get their correct meanings, and try to remember them.

• And when in doubt, go right to the horse's mouth—the supervisor—for guidance about what should be remembered about the job and about the firm's red tape, regulations, and customs. It is an important part of the supervisor's job, and he should pass along such information by easy stages. If he doesn't volunteer it, ask for it as you get an opportunity.

Although each job, and each firm, has its own special lingo and procedures, there are many things worth remembering which are about the same on all jobs. You can find a list of these on pages 126 to 132 of the second edition of our book *Practical Business Psychology.*

The breaking-in—or getting-used-to—period is usually drawn out because there are more details to be remembered than the memory can retain in a single day. Instead of trying to remember the layout of the entire plant the first day, make it a goal to get familiar with the layout of your own department, and with the route from the parking lot to the department. This goal can be on-going, so you extend your familiarity with other parts of the plant area by area, and day by day—in easy stages, but on-going.

Instead of trying to remember every face in the clattering cafeteria the first day, make it a goal to get acquainted with the names and faces of the workers nearest you on the job. Make this on-going by adding a few more day after day.

Make catching-on simple by
- (a) setting piece-by-piece goals which
- (b) are on-going and will eventually cover the entire job, and then the business as a whole.

Will this new employee have high motivation for learning the business? (Courtesy the Connecticut Mutual Life Insurance Company. From their booklet "Growing Pains," copyright 1957)

The weakness for letting remembering happen as it will is what draws out the breaking-in period more than anything else. As one provoked supervisor put it: "The new workers all give the same answer: 'Oh! I didn't think I was supposed to remember that!'"

It was partly the supervisor's fault. He should have given

some tips about what should be remembered, and told the new workers to try to remember. He should also have guided them to set for themselves some definite, close-at-hand, and on-going goals about things to remember to get on top of the job quickly.

Next we turn to General Rule II: React actively and fully to the experience you should remember, which in turn increases the effectiveness of your mental set to remember.

RULE II

React actively to the experience; look, listen, talk, think about it at the time it occurs

---

CHAPTERS:

CHAPTER 6

How reactivity helps your remembering

1. They did not react adequately

There is a saying that what matters is not what happens to a man, but what he does with what happens to him.

That applies full force to remembering. We don't remember things merely because they take place around us, but because we react to them when they happen. Some instances of people who did not remember illustrate this.

Short, full-bearded William James, first psychologist at Harvard, had to give a talk to an élite group. He was ill at ease about having to face the audience of intellectual aristocrats. Upon the advice of a friend, he took a stiff drink of whisky to brace him for the ordeal. He reported afterward that the drink helped him forget his nervousness, but that it also made him forget parts of his speech.

An office manager, recuperating from influenza, propped himself up in bed and studied a report on proposed changes in accounting methods. The next day he could recall only a few of the proposals he had studied.

A young sales executive had been kept awake much of the night by his child's illness, and felt worn out when he got to the office. Early that afternoon he dictated another batch of letters. Before he had finished the first paragraph the stenographer timidly interrupted him with her soft Southern voice: "Oh, I believe, sir, you dictated that letter this morning." Then he found he could recall scarcely any of the letters he had composed that forenoon when his reactivity had been low from loss of sleep.

A rush order in the foundry kept the lead man working harder than usual, and he was so tired he said his head buzzed. Just before change of shift his wife telephoned, asking him to stop on the way home and buy three items. When he reached the shopping center he could recall only the poison ivy remedy, and had to telephone his wife to ask what the other items were. He had forgotten them within a half hour, but it had not occurred to him that he should apply the Commonsense Rule and write them down when his wife called.

In those examples each person's reactivity had been lowered by temporary physical conditions, and remembering slumped as a result. The level of reactivity is also raised, or lowered, by our moods, interests, motives, work or study methods, even by our style of life.

This problem of reactivity—of responding adequately to the happenings we want to remember—brings us squarely to the fundamental basis for all remembering.

2. How the nervous system remembers

There is a dictum which says that we have to make an adequate reaction to anything if we are to remember it well enough to recall it later.

About the simplest reaction we can make is barely to notice what is happening—"out of the corner of the eye," or by paying little attention to it. That may be enough reactivity to remember it for a moment or two, but not much longer.

The more fully we react to any experience, the better the chances that we can recall it when we need to. The reaction is considered more likely to be adequate for remembering when we (a) react several times, (b) react for a long time, (c) react with personal interest, or (d) when we glean some meaning from the experience.

An adequate reaction is needed to make an impression in the nervous system. What is impressed are some biochemical changes. All that is stored up in memory are some intricate and rapidly occurring chemical changes in living cells which seem to work somewhat as electronic valves do. There are no "miniature pictures" stored up, as was believed a century ago.

The simplest remembrance involves biochemical changes in thousands of nerve cells. The cells which hold the traces of a single memory are scattered through many parts of the brain. It is quite likely that a single nerve cell will be included in the circuits of several different memories; this could account for some of the incorrect recalls we make, and should lead us to be wary of any pushbutton memory scheme based on trick associations of ideas.

How securely any memory is retained depends upon how adequately we have reacted to the experience. This will become clearer as we take an excursion into the laboratory to look at the waves of electricity which our brains give off as they are working.

3. What the brain waves show about reactivity

Bursts of electrical waves are being given off from the brain every moment of our lives. These brain waves, discovered by Dr. Hans Berger after thirty years of research, are altered as the processes in the brain cells shift from moment to moment. The brain-wave changes provide the most accurate inside information about reactivity in the head.

(a) During *deep sleep* the brain waves are at their slowest. Only two or three waves a second, and reactivity is near rock bottom.

Anything that happens to or around us when our reactivity is that low cannot be recalled later. Conclusive experiments by Dr. Charles W. Simon show that nothing is remembered from a phonograph record played in our ears when we are in deep sleep. No reactivity, no memory.

(b) When we are *on the verge of going to sleep* the waves are not as slow as in deep sleep, indicating a little more chemical activity in the brain. So we are slightly reactive when on the brink of sleep. Dr. Simon found that people could recall correctly the next morning a few of the things said to them when they had been on the verge of sleep.

How little remembering there is for what occurs in this drowsy condition is shown by the way we forget most of what we read while going to sleep. One businessman says that is the cheapest time to read. He reads himself to sleep with mystery stories, and can read the same story a dozen times, for it seems like a new story at each bedtime reading.

(Chart, p. 57, is from a report by W. H. Emmons and C. W. Simon in the *American Journal of Psychology*, 1956, vol. 79, page 77. Courtesy the authors, and Dr. Karl M. Dallenbach, editor.)

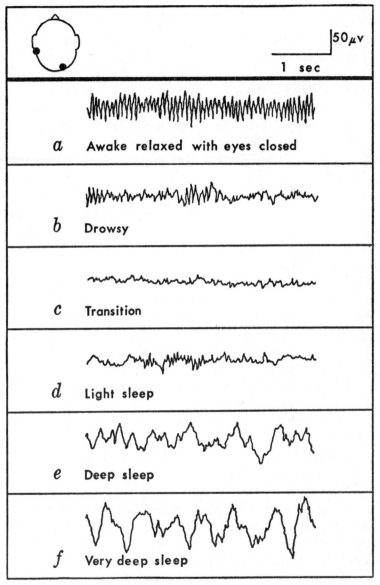

The EEG from Wakefulness to Deep Sleep.

Read yourself to sleep all you want to, but don't expect that reading to add much to your store of memories.

(c) When we are *awake, but lying relaxed,* with closed eyes and drifting thoughts, the waves are a little faster, purring along at the rate of about ten times a second for the average adult (slower than this with very young children and very old people). This relaxed rate is a landmark which is called the *Berger rhythm* of the brain.

The faster waves when one is lying relaxed, but awake, indicate more reactivity than when drowsy. We are able to remember more of what happens. But we are not yet reactive enough for memory to be hitting on all cylinders, as relaxed churchgoers discover when they are asked what the sermon was about.

(d) If, while lying relaxed as described above, you simply open your eyes to *look at something,* your reactivity perks up sharply. The instant you actively look at something, the brain waves speed up. This increase in speed reflects the fact that you are now beginning to react intentionally to something that is going on around you.

This is about the least reactivity one can have when up and around with eyes open, but it is enough to bring about a sizable increase in how much one remembers. But at this level of reactivity a large share of it will be quickly forgotten. We would guess that the office manager had about this level of reactivity as he read the accounting report in bed.

All day long the brain waves are changing speed; their voltage (which is infinitesimal) and their general pattern also change; now active in one part of the brain, later in another part. It isn't exactly correct, however, to say that they are changing. It is more accurate to say that we change them as we change our attitudes of reacting.

4. A sudden change in Einstein's reactivity

The way an active attitude perks up reactivity was shown by an episode while Albert Einstein's brain waves were being recorded. His waves were being recorded while he worked at a mathematical problem which was easy routine for him, although it would have stumped lesser mortals. It was a real problem in connection with his researches, not a make-believe problem.

As he worked at it his brain waves jogged along at a moderate canter, indicating he was not much more than moderately reactive. He could recall all the mathematics needed for the routine problem without having to rack his brains. So his waves jogged along at the leisurely pace that is customary when one is somewhat passive.

Then suddenly his waves began to gallop headlong, and became pronounced in some regions of his brain. He discovered he had made a mistake. At once he pulled himself together alertly, which means that he increased his reactivity. The shifting of his brain waves reflected his more active frame of mind.

When it seemed easy to him, he worked rather passively. But as soon as he ran into the challenge, he gave up passiveness and his brain waves began to march in double time and in new directions.

His experience highlights several points which apply to all people, from geniuses to the feebleminded:

> We are likely to loaf along with only moderate reactivity until motivated by some challenge, special interest, goal, or ambition.
>
> But we can voluntarily increase our reactivity to a worthwhile extent.
>
> As we increase our reactivity, the brain waves and brain-

cell activity shift in step, and the nervous system is tuned
up to be better able to make traces of new impressions,
or to revive the traces of older impressions we want to
recall.

5. Why people differ in reactivity

Everyday observations warrant the belief that some people are generally more reactive than others. Some well-
known personages illustrate this.

President Theodore Roosevelt could be called highly reactive. As a young man he adopted the strenuous life, osten-
sibly to overcome his physical weakness. He breezed through
life with a bounce, vigor, dash, and enthusiasm which became his trademark. He was absorbingly interested, or effec-
tively pretended he was, in everything he tackled.

His high reactivity—responding intently to what happened around him—is reflected in the many incidents
which are told about his ability to remember. Such as the
day he made an inspection of a hospital in New York City,
and was introduced individually to each of the thirty physi-
cians at the start of the day. That afternoon, on leaving, he
shook hands with each of the thirty and called him by the
correct name. At the time of this incident he was past the
prime of life, a period when brain waves slow down and
most people have more and more difficulty remembering
names and faces.

President Woodrow Wilson was chilly in comparison. He
was outwardly much less reactive than Teddy. Wilson was
slower-moving, kept his enthusiasms concealed, appeared
bored by much he had to do, and inclined toward a quiet
life which gave him the length of time he wanted for thinking anything through.

Wilson's lesser reactivity was reflected in a much less impressive memory than Roosevelt's. Wilson's memory for names and faces was probably no better than average. For remembering what he had read, or what he wanted to put in a letter, he played safe and made detailed notes (as we recommended in Chapter 2). Dr. William B. Scott, a long-time associate, said that Wilson wanted things in writing because of his distrust of memory.

Wilson held himself in check—low reactivity.

Teddy let himself go, or perhaps made himself go until it became a habit—higher reactivity.

No laboratory studies have been made so that we can say that one person is, say, 25 per cent more reactive than another. But from what Dr. David Weschler has discovered about individual differences in general, it is safe to presume that the most reactive person is about two or three times more so than the least reactive person. That is the usual range in differences between the top and the bottom in normal human capacities. It is also the range between the best man and the poorest man in tests of memory.

Such differences in reactivity may be partly inborn. The basic brain-wave rate, or Berger rhythm, is ten per second for the average adult. But for some it is a slow six, for others a speedier twelve or fourteen. This rhythm, which is a trademark of a person during his prime of life, reflects what may be called his basic level of reactivity. To that extent, then, differences in reactivity are inborn.

Mental specialists share the opinion, however, that the style of life a person chooses to live—such as T.R.'s strenuous life—has much to do with his reactivity, and can slow down or speed up his brain waves significantly.

Some people have the habit—or style—of taking life pas-

HOW MILD CRITICISM HARMED EASY HEADWORK

Seconds to do
one work unit:

How Mild Criticism Harmed Easy Headwork. Fifty men and women were timed while they translated short sentences into an easy code. From time to time they were given mildly critical remarks. These slight criticisms slowed every one of them down, by 8 per cent on the average. And after the critical comments they made 55 per cent more errors. (Data from experiments by Drs. Arthur W. Combs and Charles Taylor)

sively, even timidly. They almost seem to shrink from reacting to things around them.

Others have the habit—or style—of coping zestfully with whatever comes along. They usually like to have a lot coming; if it doesn't come, they go out looking for it.

Dr. D. Ewen Cameron was one of the first to emphasize that those who hold themselves in check, or are nervously preoccupied with their thoughts or worries, do not react adequately enough to passing events to remember them well. As a result, they have poor memories to add to their lists of real or imagined worries.

Another example is the way criticism of a person is likely to cause him to hold his reactivity in check, with undesirable results on how efficiently he remembers. The chartoon shows what one experiment found about this effect.

Thus the reactivity an individual shows is probably based partly on some inborn characteristics, and partly on habits and attitudes he has picked up in a more or less accidental fashion.

Fortunately, it is possible for a person to organize his life so that he can increase and direct his reactivity. This may not change his basic brain rhythm, but it will do a great deal to enable him to go through life with eyes and ears wider open, and his brain cells will react more adequately to the events of daily life. The net result: more stored away in useful form in his memory traces.

There is the simple matter of warming-up, for instance. This is important in our reactivity at any moment, but is usually overlooked. We will start with this in the next chapter as we turn to ways and means for being reactive when we should be reactive.

CHAPTER 7

Ways to warm up reactivity and remember better

---

1. WARMING-UP IS USUALLY NEEDED
2. HELPS FOR WARMING-UP
3. WARMING UP WHEN STARTING THE DAY
4. SOME OTHER APPLICATIONS IN BUSINESS
5. PHYSICAL CONDITIONS WHICH AFFECT REACTIVITY

1. Warming-up is usually needed

This morning at breakfast:

A few thousand people couldn't remember whether they had put sugar in their coffee, and had to taste it to find out.

Thousands tuned in their radios to listen to the weather report, but two minutes later couldn't recall what had been forecast.

Why all that quick forgetting? Because we remember only when we react adequately to what is happening, and reactivity is often sluggish and inadequate in the morning until one is warmed up.

There are many times later in the day, too, when reactivity becomes sluggish for reasons we will understand shortly.

These slumps make remembering and mental work inefficient at the time. Those are times when we need to warm up our reactivity.

Everyone is familiar with the physical warming-up an athlete does just before a contest. His warming-up does more than merely limber his muscles. It also warms up the nerve pathways he will use in the game. When the nerves are thus warmed up, they can be activated suddenly to make a speedy coordination when it is needed—and he is less likely to be caught asleep on second base.

With mental activities, too, the nerve paths and centers have to be warmed up to raise our reactivity to a suitable level if we are to be efficient in thinking or remembering. This warming-up, getting into the swing of it, may even be more essential for mental work than for physical skill.

2. Helps for warming-up

Warming-up is especially needed for the kind of remembering that is done when we study or read seriously. It takes fifteen minutes or longer to get warmed up to a particular topic so that usable memory traces are left in the nervous system. During that first quarter hour of reading we do not remember as well as later.

Hence it is wise after about the first fifteen minutes to back up and refresh yourself on what you read before you were warmed up on the subject matter. Once you do this you'll be amazed at how much had slipped from you in that short, cold time.

After a radio set is warmed up, it can be shifted from one station to another without a second warm-up. Human reactivity, however, is more specialized and not that adaptable.

We lose much, but not all, of our warming-up when we

change to a distinctly different topic. If we study tax rulings for an hour, then turn to analyzing the operation of a machine tool, we have to warm up anew on the second subject. And, again, we need to check back after about fifteen minutes to refresh ourselves on what we read before we were really warmed up on the machine tool.

The fact that mental warming-up is rather specific poses some problems for executives who have to switch from one topic to another many times during a day. To do this efficiently they need a rather high level of general reactivity to avoid half-cocked decisions. The best executives allow themselves a little more time to warm up so they can recall more essential details and avoid being half-cocked.

> Whenever you have to make a decision on a topic which you had not been thinking about, devote a few extra minutes to warming up your memories that bear on the topic before giving your decision.

Warming-up helps when recalling old memories, even those as familiar as addition or subtraction. The housewife who is totaling the month's accounts finds it easier to recall what 7 plus 8 is after she has been adding a few minutes. She is probably just about at the top of her warming-up for it when the job is finished, so she really doesn't have a chance to gain much from warming-up in this instance.

It is a bit different with students who are taking examinations. Even well-prepared students fumble for the answers until they "get in gear," until they are warmed up. But examinations are usually long enough so the students can gain from their warming-up. Most students have noticed that the second half of an examination is easier than the first half; the warming-up makes the second half seem easier.

Warming-up takes longer when one is trying to recall an

old memory that is not as familiar as addition or subtraction. Try to recall the names of people you met at a convention last month, for instance.

At the first try only a few names will come back. And many of them will be slightly incorrect, such as Neilson instead of O'Neill. But after getting warmed up, more and more names will come back, and they will more likely be correct.

In addition, the warming-up is most effective when done on the same kind of material you will want to impress, or to recall. Sweeping the sidewalks would not warm up the housewife for adding household accounts. Working a crossword puzzle would not be a useful warming-up for remembering freight rates.

> Warm up on the actual material whenever possible, always checking back to refresh yourself on what was covered while you were still cold on the material.

The need for warming-up will probably increase after the prime of life is over. Brain waves slow down in later years, and the plasticity of the nervous system seems to be lowered.

3. Warming up when starting the day

As someone observed, what kind of a day can you expect when it starts with getting up in the morning?

Reactivity is low for most everyone during the first hour after getting up. For a few people it is two or three hours; they don't really get going until late in the forenoon.

On first getting up we are able to do such habitual things as brush teeth, dress, eat breakfast. But habitual acts do not require much reactivity, and we can still be groggy with sleep and not recall two seconds later what we just did—that sugar in the coffee, for example.

Researchers in nerve physiology describe this period of the day as one of slow reactivation, of slow alerting of nerve centers which have to become vigilant before we are clear-headed for thinking or remembering.

Tests by Dr. Philip Worchel have shown that people cannot remember as well shortly after waking up as they do after they have been up long enough to be warmed up. These findings are confirmed every work morning by the people who hurry off to work in a haze of cobwebs, leaving their lunches or briefcases at home.

Some have learned to insure against the low reactivity of this time of day. Before going to bed they hang their briefcases on front doorknobs, where they will be bound to see them the next morning. It is also good insurance, as well as timesaving, to lay out the night before all the clothes, papers, and such which will be needed in the morning's groggy rush.

It was Benjamin Franklin's lifelong practice to stand nude at an open window and take deep breaths of cold morning air to warm up his general reactivity on first getting up. It probably helped.

Daniel Webster's daily warming-up practice may strike some moderns as even more severe than Franklin's. Webster simply got up early, often before the dawn's early light. This gave time for Nature to warm him up in her own course while his competitors were still sleeping.

Those people who need several hours to warm up mornings—perhaps one person out of four—can take out additional insurance by scheduling routine work for the first couple hours. We have just learned that such habitual acts do not require much reactivity, and can also be performed without calling much on memory.

There are other times besides getting-up time when we may need to shake off sleepiness to be reactive enough to use our heads. Research, especially that by Dr. Nathaniel Kleitman, has shown that our waking hours are punctured by waves of sleepiness. These sleepy spells occur about every two to three hours during the day, depending upon the length of the individual's cycles of sleep-and-wakefulness. At these times a person may feel like taking a nap. Or the wave of sleepiness may be less marked and he notices only some difficulty trying to keep his mind on his work. He may merely "feel tired" for a few minutes, although he has been doing nothing that is particularly fatiguing.

Usually this waking-time wave of sleepiness is over within fifteen minutes or so. After it passes over we have to warm up again. Thus we have, in effect, to start the day over on a smaller scale every two to three hours. There is more detailed information about these cycles of sleep-and-wakefulness, and also on early morning grogginess, in our book *Sound Ways to Sound Sleep.*

4. Some other applications in business

Conferences held the first thing in the morning are likely to be under a handicap. Many of the participants are merely tepid, not yet warmed up. They are therefore unable to bring to mind some of the points they could report an hour later. Their brightest thoughts come from memory after the meeting is adjourned.

Some executives insure against this by writing notes the day before to remind themselves of the points they want to make next morning.

In addition, some of the points agreed upon at the meeting may slip the minds of the participants—especially those who have been up and around only long enough to build up a lukewarm reactivity. Insure against this by distributing written summaries of the decisions reached.

Experienced conference leaders sometimes use stunts aimed to warm up the participants at the start of the day. This is done especially with sales groups whose meetings come before the store doors open, or before the salesmen go out on their routes. Group singing, marching around the room, shouting the month's slogan in unison, are common stunts. These may help wake up the participants, but may or may not activate the nerve pathways and centers needed to absorb the business of the meeting.

Free coffee is sometimes passed around, but it takes some fifteen minutes for this to become effective, and by that time the session may be over.

The individual worker is almost always faced with similar needs to warm up at the start of the work day—unless he got up early enough to be activated before he left home. What can a person do about this? Four things:

> The night before, plan the work for the first hour of the next day; write out this plan so you will not have to risk recalling it the next morning.
>
> Schedule first-hour work which will not demand much recalling or retaining.
>
> Jump right into the work, as the most efficient way to warm up, but after the first quarter hour check back to refresh yourself and to check the accuracy of what you have done.
>
> Try earnestly to remember the things you judge to be worth remembering, which is another direct way of warming up.

5. *Physical conditions which affect reactivity*

Most *diseases* lower reactivity, and remembering of all varieties is affected unfavorably. This is true for slight ailments, such as the common cold. The office manager recuperating from influenza was an example.

Fatigue lowers reactivity. Dr. Herman Ebbinghaus, who originated the experimental study of memory, found that it took him 12 per cent longer to memorize at 7 P.M. than it did at 10 A.M. when he was not fatigued. The memory span usually becomes shorter as the day progresses. The foundryman who forgot the shopping list may illustrate this.

Fatigue effects usually begin to appear after one or two hours of steady mental application. The length of time depends upon the person, and the kind of mental work he is doing. It is part of the art of personal efficiency to recognize when memory fatigue begins to set in, and to take a brief rest pause, after which an intentional effort should be made to warm up again.

Loss of sleep lowers reactivity, and with it remembering is lowered. In tests for the U.S. Army Institute of Research, Dr. Charles F. Gieseking and colleagues found that the loss of two nights' sleep was almost as bad in this respect as going without sleep for four nights. But the loss of even a few hours on one night shows up in the next morning's remembering, as was the case with the young sales executive with the sick child.

Staying up late to cram for an examination is a risky way to prepare for it.

The first day of *menstruation,* and sometimes the day before that, seems to lower the reactivity of some women.

Alcohol, even in moderate amounts, generally causes poor retention and shortens the memory span while the alcohol is in the system. William James could testify to that.

Continued heavy use of alcohol sometimes produces a chronic condition in which memory traces do not seem to be formed for recent experiences; these people have to call on their imaginations in place of their memories of recent happenings.

Old age usually brings about lowered reactivity, and with it a poor memory for recent events. Old people may forget what they have just said, and say it over again to play safe. Dr. Jeanne Gilbert tested people who were in their sixties, and compared them with others in their twenties. Those in their sixties recalled 40 per cent less of what they had just been reading. The chartoon shows how older people also remember less about the movies they have watched.

When the aged are given suitable hormones and vitamins, tests show that their remembering is usually improved. But the improvement lasts only as long as the pills or injections are kept up. However, this does not mean, as some newspapers have headlined, that there is such a thing as a "memory pill."

Insufficient *vitamin B's*, regardless of age, tend to lower reactivity. In this instance, remembering is usually improved when appropriate vitamins are added to the diet. No improvement in remembering should be expected unless the individual had a shortage of the vitamins in his regular diet.

Coffee, tea, and cola drinks contain chemicals which are similar and which stimulate reactivity for from one to four hours after taking. When used in large amounts, however, they often tend to interfere with remembering.

"Pep pills" (amphetamines, benzedrine, etc.), which can be legally bought only on prescription, tend to step up reactivity and to improve remembering when taken in small doses. When taken in large doses they produce erratic results and mental confusion. They are sometimes prescribed for people who are sluggish about getting warmed-up in the morning.

Aspirin apparently has no effects on reactivity, although

it may keep mild pains from distracting a person from his mental work.

Interesting to know about, but not likely to affect you, is the finding of Dr. R. K. Andjus that when the body temperature is lowered severely, retention is also greatly lowered.

Memory score

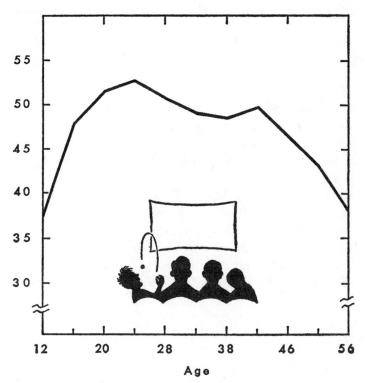

Age

How well they remembered a motion picture depended partly on how old they were. (Data from experiments on 765 people, by Dr. Harold E. Jones of the University of California)

All in all, but for having a balanced diet, maintaining good health, and avoiding fatigue and loss of sleep, there is not much the individual can do to improve his reactivity by physical means. But that much can make a big difference.

There is also the encouraging fact that methods for mentally warming up, combined with a continued earnest attitude of applying oneself to remembering, have done a great deal to increase reactivity and efficient remembering.

Dr. S. Weir Mitchell, famous neurologist, physiologist, and novelist at the turn of the century, wrote to his friend and admirer Sir William Osler: "Why is it that my brain at age seventy-five is still improving when all else of me is too clearly failing?"

We can allow for a little elderly bragging in Dr. Mitchell's description of himself. But his subsequent ten years of life were mentally more productive than the combined work of a half-dozen average people still in the prime of physical reactivity.

The answer to Dr. Mitchell's question is probably that from boyhood he, like Teddy Roosevelt, had been a mentally reactive person. He kept jumping into mental work with full force and with zest, which warmed him up quickly.

In the following chapter we will examine several other ways by which reactivity for remembering can be increased.

CHAPTER 8

Techniques for reacting several times

1. Dr. Schweitzer helped the natives remember

One elementary way for making an adequate reaction is to react several times to what you want to remember. When Dr. Albert Schweitzer, later winner of a Nobel Peace Prize, went to the tropical Congo his patients could not read. How could he be sure a native would remember the directions for taking medicine?

First, Dr. Schweitzer explained how to use the medicine, until the native understood. Then he had the native repeat the instructions ten times. That was the same method Dr. Schweitzer had used when he began the study of medicine at the age of thirty—to react several times by repeating the immense number of details he had to remember from the medical books.

Adults sometimes think it is childish to repeat in order to remember. Yet one reason why grown-ups fail to remember names, errands, appointments, and what they read is that they react only once. Repetition is an indispensable memory aid for all ages. That is one reason why advertisers spend millions saying the same thing over and over again.

Good remembering requires more than a once-over-lightly. It is seldom a single-shot proposition.

> Make your reactions more adequate by repeating what you want to remember.

2. *It helps to react several times*

We can get an idea of how repetition can aid us by making some estimates, based on laboratory tests, of how much Dr. Schweitzer helped those Congoese remember about their medicines.

If he had done nothing but tell a native how to take the medicine, a large share of them would have forgotten before reaching their native villages.

Most people listen passively to instructions, with the least possible reaction. Part of the instructions may actually not be heard. Remembering is near rock bottom under those conditions—in one ear and out the other.

As soon as Dr. Schweitzer asked the natives to repeat the instructions, they became active—much more reactive than when they were only listening. Laboratory checks have shown that merely repeating once in your own voice what you have just heard increases the amount you remember by from 25 to 100 per cent.

Each repetition after the first one adds something to the traces that are being formed. The first few repetitions usually add proportionately more than do later repetitions.

Don't jump to the conclusion, however, that the later

repetitions are a waste of time. They aren't. They make the memory longer-lasting and more readily recalled. Prepare yourself to recall it next month, and repeat it a few more times.

> It pays to overlearn by repeating more times than the minimum needed to recall it just now.

By having the natives repeat the instructions ten times, they probably remembered some four to five times better than if they had reacted only by listening in the usual passive fashion while the White Chief told them how to take the pills. (So far in this chapter we have mentioned Dr. Schweitzer eight times, to help you remember the name without trying. Had you reacted more actively, as by saying his name aloud only once, and with the intention of remembering it, chances are that you would have remembered it as well as by passively looking at it eight different times.)

3. Spread out your reactions

We remember better when our repeating, or reactions, are made in spurts instead of in unbroken runs.

Those Congoese might have remembered as much as seven or eight times better if they had repeated the instructions five times at first, and another five times an hour later. This is because the boost to remembering is almost always greatest when the repetitions are spaced apart in batches, not all at once.

You will remember a new address better, for instance, if you repeat it at odd times during the day. The odd times spread out, or space, your reactions to it.

This is applied in the old stand-by *three-times rule* for learning new words, people's names, etc. Simply use it at three *different times* during one day. This is often systematically applied by using two-faced cards which assure you that it will be correct.

4. Use two-faced cards

The pharmacist who became the world's authority on the prehistoric civilizations of Egypt and the Middle East taught himself eleven languages by using (a) the three-time rule, and (b) two-faced cards.

Dr. James H. Breasted wrote the foreign word on one side of a card, the English meaning on the other side. He carried these two-faced cards in his pocket, and at odd moments throughout the day he shuffled and studied them.

Similar two-faced cards and the three-time rule can be used for memorizing formulas, technical terms, and facts which we want to have verbatim. Some people use them for impressing names and faces, writing the name on one side and a brief description of the person's appearance, interests, etc., on the other side.

When used for new words, the most efficient procedure is to start by looking at the side which has the new word on it. After some familiarity has been gained with the new word, the cards can be flipped over to look at the meaning while you recall the word for it.

5. Applied to serious reading

Spread-out practice helps with longer material, such as serious reading. Dr. Sarah D. McAustin compared the results from rereading technical material five times in one day, with reading it once a day for five days.

A month after reading, those who had reread it five times in one day were asked to recall all they could. They recalled 11 per cent. (Amazingly little is retained by ordinary methods, even when trying to remember and reading it five times.)

But those who had spread out the rereading over five days could recall 30 per cent of the material. This was almost three times as much as the others could recall. A simple technique for more efficient remembering.

Spread-out practice usually makes all varieties of remembering more efficient. It is of most use (a) when starting a new topic, or subject, or language, (b) when the material to remember is difficult for us, or (c) when there is a great deal of material to be remembered.

Its greatest benefit is in making memories longer-lasting.

To avoid short-lived memories, space out your repetitions.

6. The value of spurts

Should we take a long wait, or a short wait, between repetitions?

We should not practice so long at one sitting that fatigue creeps in to lower our reactivity. A shorter practice session keeps us more reactive at each practice—provided we are warmed up to the material.

We do not have to be worn to a frazzle to have fatigue cut down our remembering.

Becoming bored or annoyed with all the repeating is much like fatigue in its effect. This is probably one reason why adults do not use repetition as much as they should.

By spacing out practices we will not keep at it so long at one sitting that we become bored or fatigued. We can resume the next practice with a spurt of interest, and with reactive nerve cells.

The most efficient length for practice sessions, and the best spacing between them, has to be worked out individually.

But there are some well-established guides we will turn to now.

7. *How to space your spurts*

For less difficult material that is to be learned by heart, a brief pause of two or three minutes between practices often gives the best results. This would apply to such things as addresses, price changes, names and faces, short poems, kitchen recipes.

As the material increases in length or in difficulty, the spacing between practices should be greater.

It is probably wise, however, not to space them so far apart that you skip a day. Play safe, and get some practice every day until the material is overlearned. Once you have it overlearned you can skip a day and taper off.

For the more difficult material, you can often use your feelings of fatigue or boredom as a tip-off that you have practiced long enough at that sitting.

As Amos Eaton, the lawyer who turned scientist and founded Rensselaer Polytechnic Institute, wrote his son who was starting at West Point Military Academy: "When I felt the least giddiness I stopped my studies for an hour or two. ... When my mind was confused with a subject of study, I always left it for a little jolly conversation and then resumed it with a clear head."

Parents are inclined to impose practice periods that are too long—and then wonder why the child doesn't remember much and also comes to hate practice or to dislike the subject.

Children fatigue sooner than adults, although children can stage speedy comebacks. Where a half-hour practice spell produces best results with grown-ups, we would expect a quarter hour to be more suited to a young child.

Make each practice session long enough so you get warmed up for the material.

Stop at the first sign of fatigue or boredom (but don't use this as an excuse to skimp practice on what you dread but need to remember).

When no better schedule can be worked out, use the idle moments or waiting periods of the day to react a few more times to the material.

Do not skip a day until it is nearly mastered.

There are some other unexpected factors, with odd names, which can be used to make practice more efficient, and we take up two of these next.

CHAPTER 9

Ballard and Zeigarnik can help your reactivity

1. The Ballard reminiscence effect

Dr. Philip B. Ballard was surprised to discover that London school children who had only partly memorized a poem remembered more of it the next day than they did right after their most recent practice.

One pupil remembered twenty-five lines of "The Wreck of the Hesperus" after memorizing at it on Tuesday. The next day he remembered twenty-eight lines, although he had not practiced it since Tuesday.

Gains like that, with no practice to account for them, are due to the Ballard reminiscence effect.

It is a spontaneous freshening-up of memories which has occurred with you many times. At some meeting you were introduced to six people, for example. Shortly after the introductions you recalled only four of the new names. An hour later the remaining two names popped into mind.

"Wonder how I happened to get those names now," you thought. "My mind was on something else."

Reminiscence answers your question. It is one thing we seem to get for nothing.

As with most things we get for nothing, there is a catch or two. Reminiscence occurs usually within an hour after we leave off practice, or take a rest pause in memorizing. Two days after we practice there is little, if any, boost from reminiscence. Another good reason for practicing every day —without skipping—until we have it memorized adequately, or overlearned.

How does reminiscence come about? The parlor entertainment of trying to recall the names of the states throws light on that. Dr. Warner Brown asked adults to write the names of all the states they could recall. Then he kept them occupied with something entirely different for a half hour, after which he surprised them by asking them to recall the states again.

The second time the average recalled five more states!

How was that possible? Although they had been outwardly occupied by something else meanwhile, the wheels were turning (reminiscing) in their heads and had resurrected five more states. We usually tend to keep a corner of our mental activities busy remembering for a while after we have stopped outward practice, somewhat as an automobile coasts along after we let up on the gas.

This coasting along after we stop intentional practice gives us the benefits of extra, though unintentional, practice. That is, it does if we are in a condition of reactivity that is favorable for reminiscence.

2. How to make use of reminiscence

Several conditions help us keep the wheels coasting along after we have apparently halted practice. These enable a corner of our mental activities to keep working over the material, making more useful memory traces.

Be interested in what you want to remember. Interest often pulls remembering out of a rut. This is partly because it touches off a stronger reminiscence effect than boresome material does.

Thus the teen-ager reminisces more about the names of parts of the motorcycle in which he is interested than in the names of the bones of the body which the school board thinks he should remember, more about the telephone numbers of the girls he is interested in than of the girls he considers wet blankets.

A book which is third choice in interest takes about 20 per cent more study time to remember as well as the first choice book, Dr. Edward L. Thorndike reported. He also found that pretended interest helped remembering, though not as much as spontaneous, natural interest did.

> If you lack enthusiasm for some of the things you should remember, then try working up some pretended interest for them.

Select what is useful to know. Reminiscence is greater, Dr. G. R. Martin demonstrated, when the material makes some sense to the person studying it. Or when he thinks it is worth knowing.

Dr. Thorndike made tests on remembering birth dates, which verify that. He used birth dates of famous people and of unknown people. The birth dates of the celebrities were learned two to three times better.

> Search for the significance, or usefulness, of what you have to remember, and your mind will more likely keep working on it after you have left off practicing.

Stretch yourself a bit. There is more reminiscence when the material is difficult enough to make us stretch to remember it.

In this case easy doesn't do it. If it seems easy, we are likely to skip through without trying. When it is difficult, however, we not only try harder (which always increases the amount we retain), but we are also likely to be challenged to chew it over inwardly between practices.

That is one reason why most people do not know how well they might remember. They have coddled themselves into ruts.

An illustration of the value of having to stretch came from Dr. Edward S. Robinson's tests on remembering numbers. This memory job had two handicaps; it was not interesting, and the numbers were useless to know. Dr. Robinson put a challenge in the test by steadily increasing the length of the numbers. The people he tested had to keep stretching more and more.

As the difficulty increased, the amount they recalled also increased. More stretching, more remembered.

But we learned earlier that there is a danger in stretching too much. There is, if we stretch too much too suddenly and fail. Stretch a little more each time, however, and the failing point will usually be pushed farther away. As Dr. Thorndike summed up some special experiments which he made on this:

"Work that is too hard is very bad, but not as bad as it might be."

3. Use reminiscence for muscular learning, too

Remembering which involves muscular skills, such as learning to typewrite, play a musical instrument, operate a machine, and athletic games and outdoor sports, is especially benefited by reminiscence.

Reminiscence may be helped along in these activities because they are likely to be interesting to do (except for children who are forced to practice music), seem useful to know, and also give a challenge to improve speed or score.

Thus there are motives to do imaginary practice, or make "dry runs" during the breaks between practice on these. When learning to typewrite, most people at odd moments between practices find their fingers twitching as if they were typing a sentence. That is muscular reminiscence, although it originates in the nervous system, of course, rather than in the muscles.

We have already learned that the reminiscence effect is gone after a couple days with such things as a poem, or names and faces. Luckily for our mechanized world, the Ballard effect lasts much longer—possibly for years—with muscular skills we are learning.

Weekend hobbyists who are learning a new sport illustrate that. They are often amazed that they can begin a new weekend with more skill in tennis, or what not, than they left off with the previous weekend. That unearned gain is partly the result of reminiscence in muscular memory during the six days they had no visible practice.

The old saying that we learn to skate in summer and to swim in winter is often true. But bear in mind that in the case of intellectual remembering we lose most of the Ballard benefits if we miss a day of practice.

We can take a tip from this Ballard reminiscence effect, and stretch ourselves during odd moments to do some intentional recalling of what we have recently practiced, or observed and want to remember.

4. The Zeigarnik effect when a task is unfinished

The Zeigarnik effect has such a distinctive name that it should be remembered without intentionally repeating it. We will play safe, however, and repeat it in spaced-out fashion to make the memory of it more durable.

This effect was discovered by Dr. Bluma Zeigarnik at the University of Berlin. Mrs. Zeigarnik set out to see what happened when people were kept from finishing tasks they had started. She found that they remembered the unfinished tasks some 50 per cent better than similar ones they finished without interruption.

That is one aspect of the Zeigarnik effect—*a proclivity to REMEMBER unfinished business, and to forget finished business.*

You have experienced this when you have looked up a telephone number but found the line busy when you first called it. The incompleted call is unfinished business which keeps some inner activity going on. Because of that on-going activity, you can call the number a few minutes later without having to look it up again.

But as soon as you finish the call, the number drops through a hole in memory. The business is finished, and memory of the number finished with it.

The Zeigarnik effect is also common when a person is

dictating a batch of letters. You can keep in mind what you have dictated until a letter is finished. But as soon as you turn to the next letter, you have trouble recalling how the preceding one was worded.

In posting accounts, forgetting of the details usually occurs as soon as they are posted.

The same effect is shown by card players who remember which cards have been played, but forget them as soon as the hand is finished.

Housewives remember the recipe until the pudding is put into the oven.

In Dr. Brown's test of recalling the names of the states, the people were aware they had not recalled all of them. That gave them some unfinished business, although they were outwardly occupied with something else the next half hour.

This effect may also play a part in the improved remembering when we stretch ourselves to memorize difficult or long material. That kind of material can make one keenly aware of unfinished memory work to be done.

Another aspect of the Zeigarnik effect is *a proclivity TO COMPLETE unfinished business.*

When interrupted while doing something we are interested in, our motivation to finish it is usually sharpened. We keep on reacting inwardly to the unfinished business. "Can't get it off my mind until I go back and finish it," we say.

An experience of Thomas A. Edison's, when he was twenty-six, can be taken as an example. He was standing in line to pay taxes in the Newark, New Jersey, city hall. As the long line of last-minute taxpayers inched to the window, Edison was concentrating on an invention to combine the duplex and diplex telegraphs.

When he came to the head of the line, the clerk asked for his name. That question interrupted his unfinished thinking. The interruption so strengthened his motive to finish his

A POSSIBILITY OF THE
ZEIGARNIK EFFECT.

(From the booklet "Satisfaction Guaranteed." Copyright 1958 by the Connecticut Mutual Life Insurance Company)

thoughts that he couldn't recall his name. The then-unknown inventor had to start over at the end of the line.

The schoolgirl who was called in from play to do her homework is another and more familiar example. She complained, "I can't study; all I can think about is roller skating."

Workers are generally impatient to get back to their regular jobs when they have been interrupted to help out on other jobs. If a worker has to help out temporarily on something else, he will help out more enthusiastically, and have more of his mind on the relief job, if he leaves his regular job at some natural stopping point—not in the middle of typing a letter, for instance, but after the letter has been completed.

5. How to apply the Zeigarnik effect

Each halt in practice works as an interruption. Thus we remember better after taking the rest pause in practice.

The stop is also likely to increase the proclivity to get back to the job of memorizing. When this is the case, we resume memorizing with a spurt, as if to make up for lost time and get the business finished.

The Zeigarnik effect is strongest shortly after the interruption. It almost never lasts over into the next day.

Don't wait too long between practices.

The effect may disappear within a few minutes if lively conversation takes one's mind off the unfinished business. With our telephone number example, the number will probably have to be looked up again if we become absorbed in something else before making the call again.

Do routine or uninteresting tasks in the pauses between practice spurts.

The Zeigarnik effect depends upon how much a person wants to accomplish the task. If he doesn't want to remember, or is forced by teacher or employer to go through the motions, we would not expect much Zeigarnik benefit. It is the person's own motivation to finish or remember something that makes him tick the Zeigarnik way.

The shiftless person who takes life easily and has no particular goals in view probably gets little help from this effect. When he stops practice, the wheels stop because there is no business he wants to finish. He may spread out his practice sessions, but should not expect much of a spurt when he resumes practice.

> Set up some achievement goals which are on-going and challenging so there will always be some unfinished business to motivate your remembering and keep you reactive.

Reactivity for remembering is also helped by variety, which can give spice to remembering, as we shall find in the following chapter.

CHAPTER 10

Methods for reacting several different ways

1. USE SEVERAL GATEWAYS
2. GET SUITABLE MUSCLES INTO THE ACT
3. TALK TO YOURSELF AT THE TIME
4. RECITE IT TO YOURSELF LATER

1. Use several gateways

Long before researchers decided that we remember only the things we respond to adequately, Abraham Lincoln was following that principle to teach himself law.

"I prefer to study aloud," he told his law partner. "That gives me the benefit of hearing as well as seeing what I read, and I remember it better."

Reading was strainful for him, as Dr. Edward J. Kempf has pointed out, because his left eye gave blurred images. To eliminate the strain from rereading in order to remember, Lincoln hit upon the technique of reading aloud in his high-pitched, staccato voice.

Using the two gateways—ears as well as eyes—did not necessarily double the efficiency of his remembering. We can be sure, however, that Lincoln got much more out of a single reading because he responded more fully by using two senses at the same time.

The relative merits of reading versus hearing the same material have been checked by Dr. Wilse B. Webb at the U.S. Naval School of Aviation Medicine. One way turned out as well as the other.

But when Dr. Webb had the men use eyes and ears at the same time, they comprehended much more of what they read. Multiple coverage helped.

When you want to remember something, take it in through as many senses as possible. Each sense brought into action not only increases your reactivity to the material, it also gives you an additional set of clues when it comes time to recall or recognize the material.

If you merely look at a word, will you recognize it later if you hear it? The appearance would be familiar, but not the sound.

If you only hear a person's name, you risk not being able to say it later.

> Make a diversity of connections at the start, including all the gateways through which you may want to revive the memory traces later.

2. Get suitable muscles into the act

Muscles make better gateways than you may imagine. There are several senses in our muscles, tendons, and joints, but they are usually left out of the act when we try to remember. This is a real loss, because memories which are tied in with muscle senses tend to be unusually long-lasting.

John R. Commons, the famous labor economist, worked his way through college setting type. Forty years after he had last set type he visited a printing office and tried to recall where the letters were stored in the type case. He couldn't recall their location.

Then he tried to set some type. He let his fingers follow their inclinations, and they at once set type correctly. The muscle senses remembered after forty years, although his other senses had long since forgotten.

In addition to the relative permanence of their remembering, the muscle senses are often the ones through which we are called on to express memories. When forming memories we should include the muscles through which we may have to use the memories later. This is in line with the principle that memories are most serviceable when we form them in the manner in which they will be called back later.

When reading instructions for operating a machine, for instance, put the muscles through the motions of moving the levers and switches as you read about each. Better yet, make the motions on the machine itself as you are forming the original impressions.

Sometime you will want to write that new word you are learning. Go through the motions, write it, to get the muscle senses in the act. Spelling it will be less of a hazard later.

Pronounce it aloud at the outset, too. This will lessen the chances of fumbling when you try to use it the first time in public.

3. Talk to yourself at the time

When Lincoln read aloud he did more than add the sound of the words to his memory impressions. He also got his jaws, tongue, lips, and vocal machinery into the act.

The sensations from the muscles used in talking are exceedingly useful in remembering. This may be because we tend to use our talking muscles when we do hard thinking.

Count Leo Tolstoi, the novelist and philosopher, found it

useful to talk to himself when doing mental work. At the age of eighteen he decided upon six rules to follow to make the most of his talents. Rule Number 5 was: "Always think and read aloud."

Sir Herbert Beerbohm Tree, famous actor and manager of Her Majesty's Theatre, had been in a London taxi for an hour, talking to himself in a monologue all the while. When his companion tried to say something, Sir Herbert snapped at him: "Don't talk so much; it hinders my thought. I always think aloud, and I can't stand people talking when I'm thinking at the top of my voice."

We may not talk aloud, as Tree and Tolstoi did intentionally. But we whisper to ourselves, or move the lips slightly. Or our vocal muscles make invisible motions, somewhat as the bowler's arm tenses as if swinging an imaginary ball when he thinks of the strike he made last night. This invisible and inaudible talking occurs with most of our thinking.

When something keeps us from doing this invisible talking, remembering is cut down. This was first demonstrated by Dr. M. C. Barlow, by the simple procedure of having people hold pencils between their teeth to interfere with invisible talking. They did not remember new words as well when the invisible movements had been cut down.

It works the other way. Saying it aloud, or even whispering it to oneself, improves the remembering.

How much saying it to oneself helps one remember it is suggested by experiments which Dr. Carl I. Hovland made with soldiers. (Recall his story of the men memorizing a shuffled pack of fifty-two cards?) In this test the men had to memorize the military alphabet, such as A = Able, B = Baker, C = Charlie, etc. He compared two methods for remembering.

For one method, the soldiers were shown a card reading A = Able, and the instructor read it aloud to them. This combined the gateways of seeing and hearing. The soldiers sat, looked, and listened.

For the other method, the soldiers added to their reactivity by putting their talking muscles into the act. They repeated the code themselves as each card was flashed.

The soldiers remembered from 25 to 40 per cent more when they talked to themselves at the time they were memorizing the code.

Bear that in mind when you want to remember names and faces—talk to yourself. In a laboratory test made by Dr. Harold E. Burtt, names were remembered 34 per cent better when the person repeated the name upon being introduced. Say more than "Glad to meet you." Include the name, too.

When learning some muscular skill, talk to yourself. Some dancing schools insist that students prompt themselves at the start, saying as they glide: "Two steps right, now one left, now dip." Typewriting, golf, and bowling instructors use similar talk-to-yourself techniques.

When learning to operate a machine, say to yourself what you should do next until the correct motions are thoroughly remembered.

Music while you work, or while you study, may interfere with this desirable kind of talking to oneself. The talking muscles are likely to hum the tune, or whisper the words, preventing the muscles from helping us think. An example is the check Dr. Mack T. Henderson made on the effect of music upon college students who were studying. Even the students who preferred to study with radio music tuned on softly got less out of their reading when there was music in the air.

Whatever you want to remember, talk to yourself about it at the time and you will usually have a more serviceable memory of it.

4. Recite it to yourself later

Reading aloud, as Lincoln did, does help one remember. But it is relatively inefficient because reading speed is cut practically in half.

The most efficient way to combine talking and reading is: First, read silently to get the meaning. Then, pause from time to time to recite to yourself the gist of the last few minutes' reading.

When reading and self-reciting were combined that way, Dr. Herbert F. Spitzer discovered that people recalled four times as much two weeks after the reading.

How much of the time should be spent in reciting to oneself?

When the material was brief, without much meaning, and had to be remembered verbatim, Dr. Arthur I. Gates found best results when three-fourths of the time was spent reciting to oneself.

For longer and more meaningful material (such as this book), Dr. Harvey A. Peterson reported best results when only about a third of the time was spent reciting the gist of it to oneself.

The least efficient time to recite to oneself is after the reading, or chapter, is finished. It is most efficient to interrupt the reading every few minutes to explain it to oneself. The interruption may give a bonus by touching off a Zeigarnik effect.

For the usual serious reading, the best timing would probably be to read silently and speedily for the meaning for three to five minutes. Then pause to recite, or whisper, to yourself for a minute or two about the substance of what was just read, and to tie it in with what was read ten minutes earlier.

In this book, for instance, the breaks between topics in a chapter provide ready-made places to pause and recite what was in the section. Most nonfiction has such natural breaks. Use them as signals to react fully by pausing to recite to yourself.

Another signal to pause-and-recite comes at any point where you have difficulty understanding the meaning. Talk to yourself about the troublesome point, until it clears up and you can explain it to yourself; you may need the help of a dictionary to do this. If you read blithely ahead without clearing up the meaning, your comprehension of what follows may be so diluted that the memory will be of no use— like Lonnie's in Chapter 1.

Tests show that one person will get as much out of reading only once through as another does after reading three times. We can be pretty sure which of them responded several different ways in their reading.

We will now leave the question of reacting fully to form the most efficient impression and turn to General Rule III, which deals with methods for keeping the impression fresh so that forgetting is cut down.

RULE III

*Refresh your memories at strategic times
to keep them accurate and from going stale*

CHAPTERS:

CHAPTER 11

Ways to cut down forgetting

1. WHAT YOU ARE LIKELY TO FORGET
2. YOU FORGET RAPIDLY AT FIRST
3. THEN FORGETTING SLOWS DOWN
4. BUT YOU CAN ALWAYS RELEARN MORE RAPIDLY THAN YOU FORGET

1. What you are likely to forget

We have learned so far about techniques which help impress things in memory by having a favorable mental set, and by reacting adequately. Next, and now, come the strategies for keeping what we have impressed from going stale.

"My memory," the little girl said, "is what I forget with." She was more nearly correct than her parents realized as they laughed at her.

Forgetting sets in a few seconds after anything is learned. It usually trots briskly downhill from then on. As a consequence of this rapid disappearance of memories, it is essential to give more attention than is usually done to slow down the speedy forgetting.

Forgetting does not have to be the jinx in the memory cycle. A great deal can be done to cut it down. You will find some preliminary hints about how to cut it down from these lists of the things we are most likely to forget.

Most forgetting of
Names (of things as well as of people)
Numbers and dates
Unpleasant things
What is learned barely enough to remember it
Facts at odds with our beliefs or prejudices
What we learn by cramming
Our failures
What we pick up incidentally without trying to remember it
Things we think of only once or twice after memorizing them
Material we don't understand
What we try to remember when embarrassed, frustrated, in poor health, or fatigued

Least forgetting of
Pleasant experiences
What we review before going to bed
Things that seem to us worth remembering
What we give time to sink in before going further
Things we talk about often
Long or difficult material we stretch ourselves to learn
Material we review, or think about often
Facts and topics that interest us
Our successes
Material that makes sense to us
Memories tied in with muscular skills
What we use most frequently
What we had a motive to remember for a long time when we were first learning it

2. You forget rapidly at first

Newspaper reading provides a good example of the speed with which we forget. By the time the average reader reaches page 5 he already has trouble recalling what he read on the front page. More slips away than sticks, as is true of all our casual remembering.

Why this almost instantaneous forgetting of the larger share of our daily experiences?

For one thing, we forget because we do not try to remember. We merely read, not reacting fully enough to remember it two pages later.

But even when we do react more, and do try to remember things, we do not give each enough time to "sink in." In the newspaper we read many items, one right after the other. The items read on page 2 erased some of the memory traces of what was read on page 1 before the page 1 impressions had time to "jell."

(Exactly how impressions jell in the nervous system is still a puzzle. The trend of biochemical studies of the brain would suggest that protein molecules, and enzymes and coenzymes which operate on the molecules, are involved. Until the exact nature of the memory trace is better understood, the everyday phrase "to jell" will help us visualize that some trace is made which needs time to become stable, and which can be wiped out by conditions unfavorable to its permanence.)

Back to that newspaper we were reading before being interrupted by chemistry. The principal items we remember from page 1, or any other page, are those which struck our fancy enough to make us pause a few moments to think about them. That pause, and the added reaction of thinking about them, let them sink in a bit and become partly erase-proof before the next items came along to erase them.

But even when we do give them time to sink in, after a couple weeks more is likely to be forgotten than remembered. Consider these typical examples of the speed with which people forgot material which seemed worth remembering, and which they tried seriously to remember.

Sixth-grade children studied a two-page informative article, knowing they would be asked questions about it. Dr. Herbert F. Spitzer checked what they remembered of the article immediately after reading it, and again in two weeks.

Two weeks later they had forgotten 80 per cent of what they had remembered immediately after studying the article.

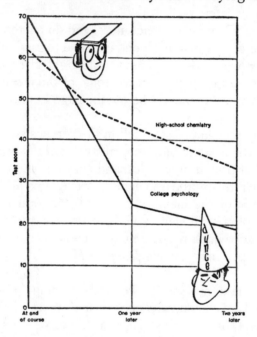

School Training Fades Rapidly. (Data from Dr. S. L. Pressey)

Adults do not do any better, by and large. In one case adults studied technical material, and had the advantage of studying it through five times within a single day. The day after studying it, Dr. Sarah D. McAustin found, the average could recall only two-thirds of the information he had read five times.

Two weeks later those adults had forgotten 80 per cent of what they had remembered the day after the concentrated study.

That's the way with remembering . . . *Going* . . . Going . . . GONE!

3. Then forgetting slows down

The *Going* is enormous the first day or two.

The Going the next two weeks is bad, too.

But don't give up—the first two weeks are the worst.

The amount we remember after two weeks has a fair chance of staying much longer. It may not linger as a permanent memory unless we help it jell by procedures we will take up in the next few chapters; but at least it leaks away much more slowly after the first two weeks.

We have been looking at a negative aspect of remembering; now let's look at some encouraging factors.

4. But you can always relearn more rapidly than you forget

Even during the speedy forgetting of the first week or two we can keep ahead of the forgetting if we touch up the fading memory by a little strategic relearning.

Here is an example of what relearning can do, from the first scientific experiments on remembering, by Dr. Herman Ebbinghaus. He used the tedious memorizing of lists of meaningless syllables which resembled Chinese family names, or ticker-tape abbreviations. Each nonsense name was seen for only $\frac{2}{5}$ second. The job was to memorize 108 of these verbatim—an unpleasant job that only an inquisitive scientist would have the motivation to do.

The first day these lists had to be studied sixteen times before they were barely remembered.

By the next day so much had already been forgotten that the same lists had to be studied eleven more times to relearn them. Yet that was a saving of nearly a third of the memorizing time as compared with the first day.

The savings increased day by day. On the sixth day the lists could be recalled perfectly after only two times over them. From then on, the memory of the lists was as permanent as could be expected for such fiendish, meaningless material; but it would still have to be brushed up, say, once a month to keep it from slipping into oblivion.

When the material to be remembered is meaningful, the saving in relearning is much greater. Things that make sense for us generally need to be brushed up only three or four times altogether for the memory to come close to 100 per cent. Fortunately, a large share of our memories are meaningful. Most of them should be, if we are to remember efficiently.

Memories that we use often, such as the multiplication table or our names, seldom leave us. Each time we use them we are brushing them up, so they stay jelled permanently.

It seldom occurs to adults to do some relearning, or brushing up, to offset their rapid forgetting. But whenever it is something you should remember, better refresh yourself on it until it comes to the tip of your tongue whenever you want it.

> Keep ahead of forgetting by brushing up a memory a few times before it is two weeks old.

Leave remembering to its own course, and inevitably that course will be downhill. You will have forgetting rather than remembering as a reward for not helping the traces jell.

Now we will take up a few techniques which make the brushing-up most effective.

CHAPTER 12

Techniques for brushing up memories

1. MEMORIES REQUIRE REGULAR MAINTENANCE
2. BRUSH THEM UP EARLY
3. BRUSH THEM UP AT BEDTIME
4. BRUSH THEM UP AGAIN WITHIN A WEEK
5. HOW TO BRUSH THEM UP ACCURATELY
6. REFRESH THEM MORE THAN IS NEEDED TO GET BY

1. Memories require regular maintenance

Husky Roger Williams was an earnest freedom-fighter who taught himself the languages of the major New England Indian tribes. This Welshman's wonderful strength, square dealing, and skill with Indian languages gave him more influence than any other colonist over the savages. Time after time he got the red men to smoke the pipe of peace after they had been provoked to start on the warpath.

As he turned forty, Williams faced an easy opportunity to forget the Indian tongues. He was returning to London, to dicker for more than a year about a royal charter for Rhode Island. That would be time enough for his memories of the Indian languages to dwindle to a useless residue.

He hedged against that lapse on the slow sail across the Atlantic. He spent the time writing in an unventilated, bilge-scented cranny of the ship. Drawing solely on his fresh memory, he produced one of the first American books, titled *Key to the Language of America.* In it he gave a fairly complete account of the Indian languages of the Eastern states. Although the book was useful to other colonists, his first reason for writing it was selfish.

This pioneer book, written in the bowels of the ship, would be, he wrote, "a private helpe to my owne memory, that I might not by my absence lightly lose what I had so dearely bought in some few years of hardship among the barbarians."

Being a fighter by nature, he fought back at forgetting.

It is essential that we fight back if we expect to retain the memory of most anything. As Roger Williams suspected, memories are not long for this world unless we maintain them in freshened-up condition.

Some methods of fighting back—or brushing up—have been proven to be much more efficient than other ways.

2. Brush them up early

Don't wait for a slow boat trip to brush up your memories. The most efficient time to begin to refresh a memory is within a few minutes after it is first established. Act upon the fact that memories begin to lapse almost the instant they are formed.

Right after first learning a person's name, for instance, it will take only about three seconds to recall it correctly. Two hours later it takes a minute or longer if you have not brushed it up in the meantime. The next day it may take several tries to recall the name, and you may not be able to get it back. The day after that there are good chances that you will not be able to recall it at all, or that you will recall the wrong one.

Since all memories dissolve in that fashion, they need to be brushed up early and often. Memory is not like a camera which you snap once and it registers the image permanently. Memory has to be snapped several times. Here are some examples.

Something you have read? Tests show that it will more likely be remembered tomorrow if you stop reading after about five minutes and brush it up by reviewing in your thoughts what you have just read. Better yet, talk to yourself about it to give the traces a better chance to sink in.

Don't wait until the end of the chapter or article. Make another exposure before the section you have just read has disintegrated any further. (Do these two paragraphs sound familiar? Good! The important point is beginning to jell.)

Is it the name of a person you have just met, or a technical term just heard? Offset the speedy lapsing which occurs at the start by repeating the name in your conversation while the name is still warm.

Write it down, also, if you want to be really certain of it tomorrow.

Or ask for a calling card, or letterhead. Keep these on file, for later help which we will discuss shortly.

Is it an interview, or agreement? Many top-flight executives wind up interviews by summarizing to the other person the points they have discussed, and the actions that have been agreed upon. This wind-up not only brushes up the memory and offsets some of the rapid initial forgetting, it also makes it more certain that the other person will not draw wrong conclusions.

> Whenever you have just taken in something that is worth remembering, pause to refresh it, or use it in conversation, before going on to the next business.

Tomorrow, as we shall see, it is likely to be recalled so incorrectly that if you wait until then to brush it up you will be filling your memory with errors.

3. Brush them up at bedtime

Bedtime is one of the best times to offset forgetting.

We recall that tender young memories are likely to be wiped out before they have time to jell. This erasing is considered the main cause of everyday forgetting.

What does the erasing? Later experiences which compete with the new memories for a place in some of the same nerve pathways and switching centers. What we read on page 2 erases some of the traces of what we read on the front page, for instance.

Our own thoughts do a lot of the erasing. We have from eight to twelve thoughts a minute, but would probably be better off memory-wise if we had only one a minute. As things are, however, we may not remember the first thought by the end of the minute. It is usually wiped out by the three or four which follow it. If we want to remember the first, we have to grab it by the tail as it goes past and hold on to it—or write it down, right away.

Thus there is probably more competition, and consequent crowding-out, in memory than there is in even business or politics. The technical term for this crowding-out in remembering is *retroactive inhibition*.

There is least crowding-out during sleep, because there

are then few new experiences or thoughts to erase the young memories.

Drs. John G. Jenkins and Karl M. Dallenbach were the first to measure the benefit from bedtime memorizing. They discovered that only 9 per cent of what had been memorized in the forenoon could be recalled eight hours later. The many other experiences during the eight waking hours erased almost all the memorized material—retroactive inhibition is a fast worker.

But when similar material was memorized at bedtime, 56 per cent of it could be recalled after eight hours of sleep— retroactive inhibition was sleeping on its job.

Although it is extremely doubtful if you can learn while asleep, it is plain that just before going to sleep is a strategic time for reviewing some things you have learned during the day and want to remember.

Brush up your memories as well as your teeth at bedtime.

4. Brush them up again within a week

One secret of a "good memory" is to keep memories freshened up for their first week so they will jell rather than suffer the fate of retroactive inhibition. The first day is most critical, the first week next.

Experienced advertisers know that, and use a "crash schedule" the first week they are introducing a new product or trade name. They hammer hard and often that week at what they want people to remember.

When a leading automobile manufacturer brought out a new car recently, pictures of the car appeared in newspapers and magazines on August 27. On August 31 billboards across the country were plastered with advertisements, in time to catch the eyes of the Labor Day traffic. Three days after that, newspaper and magazine advertisements crashed in view to tell more about the car and to wind up the first week.

After that whirlwind week, the public reminders of the new car were more widely scattered. There was a wait of six weeks before television was used to brush up the public's memories of the new car.

Educators try to use a similar strategy by having reviews, or examinations, or drills, each week. Many tests show that more is remembered when there is an examination to refresh young memories each week than when the examinations are only once a month, and—the least—at the end of the course.

Many executives and professional people use the weekend for brushing up their memories of the week's significant happenings. This is a favorable time for evading the bane of retroactive inhibition. (We used that term again to brush up your memory of it while it is still young.)

The weekend solitude and slowed tempo provide almost ideal conditions for refreshing memories with least risk of their being erased by some competing experiences. There is time on a quiet weekend for a refreshed memory to jell more firmly than it might in the rush of weekday activities.

> Set up a systematic schedule for using some of your weekend time for refreshing recent memories you want to hold on to for future use.

5. How to brush them up accurately

Executives who make the fewest wild guesses in their weekend fresheners take home briefcases of notes, memos, reports, contracts, calling cards, and trade journals covering the week. These keep them on the right tracks in their brushing-up.

Almost always some objective aid is essential to keep our refreshing from being inaccurate, especially after memories are a week old and becoming incorrect in many spots, and threadbare in others.

(a) If we do the refreshing solely by what we can recall without aid, we skip many details. Unless we have some tangible guides or notes, our memories will be only partly brushed up. When we depend upon unaided recall, we brush up the parts that are already remembered, while the parts that are hard to remember (and most in need of refreshing) become weaker by the hour.

(b) If we trust solely to unaided recall when refreshing, we inevitably brush up many things inaccurately. Memories are seldom more than half accurate by the time they are a week old, as the next chapter will show us. As far as that goes, whether brushing up at the weekend or after five minutes, the problem of having the facts straight is critical.

> Check back to a written record, or to the book or article, to be sure you are not loading your memory with things that are only half-so, or even dead wrong.

Numerous tests have shown that keeping a check on accuracy, or knowing how we stand, speeds up the rate of remembering. We should keep tabs on the correctness and completeness of our brushing-up, until we reach the point where we can recall it as accurately as our own birth dates. (After you have read this chapter, you may want to turn back to Chapter 2 and refresh yourself on the fifth Commonsense Rule.)

6. Refresh them more than is needed to get by

When is it safe to stop refreshing?
Never.

You can forget anything—even your birth date—unless it is brushed up from time to time.

The common mistake is to stop trying, to ease off on reacting to it, as soon as it can be recalled easily. When that point is reached, people assume they will always remember it, and think it can be laid on the shelf to keep forever. But it is fatal to a memory to stop when you first have it in hand.

> Instead of stopping, taper off. Refresh from time to time so it becomes overmemorized.

Overmemorizing takes place for those things we use frequently, or which are a recurring part of our work. You have probably overmemorized your name, which you use, hear, see, and think about almost daily. But you may not have overmemorized your birth year, which is not used as often; life insurance companies and Social Security officials are not surprised when policyholders are off a year or two when stating the year they were born.

One of the most efficient ways of overmemorizing is to use memories in conversation. It can add to one's conversational skills, as well as keeping memories on tap.

Alexandre Dumas, author of *The Three Musketeers* and dozens of other imperishable works, overmemorized with the conversational method. He loved to talk. Luckily, he talked mostly about diverse facts he picked up here and there, and not about his opinions. People were drawn to this physical giant's fact-packed conversations. It was worth listening to him, and he won admirers at the same time he was brushing up his memories.

When you wonder what to talk about, try talking about some things you have recently picked up which you would like to remember. That can keep both your conversation and your memory from going stale.

If you don't talk about it, at least think about it, early and again at bedtime, and again within a week.

And keep accuracy uppermost.

Then you will have a jujitsu hold on your forgetting.

The problem of having accurate memories is so important that we will devote the following chapter to it.

CHAPTER 13

Know how much to trust your memory

1. The booby trap of mis-remembering

We are often booby-trapped by our "clearest" memories turning out to be very false. For example:

"There's a sneak thief in this office," the chief clerk growled as he glared suspiciously around the office.

"I had five dollars for Gertrude's wedding gift. It was right on this corner of my desk," and he whacked the corner so hard everybody in the room looked up. "I clearly remember putting it right there before I went to the stock room twenty minutes ago. Who took it?"

The clerk at the adjoining desk pointed toward the row of file cabinets. "Look on top of the Mac section," he said. "Just before you went to the stock room, you got out the file

116

on the MacPherson claim. I saw you put the money on top of the file when you needed both hands for the drawer."

Sure enough, there was the "stolen" bill, although the boss "clearly" remembered putting it on his desk. "Clearly" recalled—but it was clearly a mis-recall. Everyone considered it a good joke on the boss; they were not aware how often their own memories play similar tricks.

Mrs. Otto R. worked in the same office. Her husband worked on the other side of town. The morning the boss misremembered where he laid the bill, she and Otto remembered it was their first wedding anniversary. During breakfast they decided to celebrate with a dinner at the Chinese restaurant, and agreed to meet after work at the big store where their bus routes crossed.

He waited at the Washington Street entrance for an hour that afternoon, becoming more agitated by the minute when she did not appear. He was on the brink of starting for home alone when a friend passed.

"What's the matter? You and the wife having trouble?" the friend asked.

Otto blushed—had the friend read his mind? "What makes you ask that?" he stalled.

"Just saw her at the State Street entrance, all dolled up but looking as if she had lost her last friend—and you don't look too happy yourself."

Otto, or his wife, had slightly mis-remembered the meeting place they had decided on that morning. Each was sure he remembered it correctly, and blamed the other. Their anniversary dinner had an argumentative atmosphere that would discourage others from entering matrimony.

It would have been a happier anniversary if each had written a memo of the exact location of the rendezvous. It probably seemed so easy to remember it for only eight hours that, like most of us, they did not take that simple precaution against mis-remembering.

2. Some consequences of mis-remembering

Everyone's memory yields a large percentage of details that are mis-remembered. We may recall the high spots accurately enough, but the chances are approximately fifty-fifty that we will recall some details incorrectly, or that we will "remember" details which were not there.

Such mis-remembering can cause as much trouble as complete forgetting. Perhaps more trouble, because we almost always believe our false recalls are true blue, and blithely act upon them.

Everyday a few people are indicted for perjury because they testify on oath about details that did not agree with proven facts. Some of these witnesses, it is true, were deliberately lying and were caught at it. But we can be equally certain that others honestly thought they remembered the facts as they had testified, and were trapped by their mis-remembering.

Some of the trouble people run into with income tax auditors arises from mis-remembering.

Arguments are often started, or kept going, because one or both persons mis-remember the points about which they are disagreeing.

News that travels along the grapevine becomes unreliable because each person who passes it along usually mis-remembers a part of the gossip. After a story has been retold by a half-dozen people, it often has little resemblance to what actually happened.

Costly blunders occur in offices and factories because instructions were mis-remembered. There is ample justification for the rule to put instructions and orders in writing.

Possibly the most frequent serious consequence of mis-remembering is that it misleads judgments. A decision that is based on something one remembers as gospel truth, but which is a partly twisted recall, can be expected to be at least partly foolish.

All in all, what we forget may not make as much trouble as what we mis-recall. It is worth knowing some ways to make our memories more trustworthy.

3. How much do you mis-remember?

Tests show that anything can be mis-remembered.

Every person who has ever been tested for it has exhibited mis-remembering. It is not limited to imaginative children and hopeful fishermen.

There is most twisting, omitting, and adding in the case of memories of everyday happenings that one made no effort to remember at the time they occurred. Examples are routine transactions, names, casual reading, and all passing occurrences.

There is also some mis-remembering even when we have observed intently and studied with a deliberate effort to remember—as every student finds out when examinations roll around. The percentage of mis-remembering is smaller, however, when we observed at the time with the intention of remembering. But the mis-recalling is still so frequent and sizable that it interferes with the efficient use of what we remember.

We might expect that scientists, who have been trained to make careful observations and to stick to facts, would do little mis-remembering. This supposition was checked after a small meeting of scientists at Cambridge University where a tape recording had been made of their learned discussion. Two weeks later they were asked to report what they remembered of the meeting.

Of the things they "recalled," nearly half had not taken place.

Similar tests on people from many walks of life reveal that mis-remembering sets in almost immediately. The most accurate rememberer usually is wrong in at least one-fourth of what he recalls the same day it happened. The average rememberer is wrong in about half the details he recalls the same day—as badly off as those scientists were two weeks after the event they tried to recall.

The mis-remembering is greatest when the person tries to recall more than comes back to him at the first attempt. The first account you give of an event will usually be the most accurate, though it may cover only the skeleton of the event. As you dig deeper into memory for other details, mis-remembering increases by leaps and bounds.

Some trial attorneys, and congressional inquiries, take advantage of this weakness. They press a witness to recall additional details until he soon swears things are true which can easily be proven false, thereby giving the impression that the witness is not telling the truth.

> Don't put much faith in details you sweat to recall. Just skip them, or check back to the record and straighten out your memory.

In view of all this, even under the best of circumstances we should not trust more than one-fourth of the details we remember.

Which of the details we recall should we believe? We will find some suggestions about this in a moment.

4. Most mis-remembering in older memories

An example of how mis-remembering becomes worse as the weeks go by was shown by Winifred Davis and her lost brooch. The day the brooch was missing, mother and daughter retraced their steps to hunt for it. They inquired of every person they had seen that day, and described the brooch as a circlet about the size of a dime, with seed pearls around the edge.

A week later they advertised for it, offering a reward because of its sentimental value. In the advertisement they described it as about the size of a quarter, surrounded with medium-sized pearls. The details had grown in one week.

By the end of the year they described the still missing brooch as the size of a half dollar, of heavy solid gold, covered with gem pearls, each as large as a pea. Grown still more.

Then they unexpectedly found the brooch while rummaging in the attic. It turned out to be a tarnished circle, slightly smaller than a dime, with dots of something that looked like baby pearls around the rim.

The way mis-remembering becomes worse as time goes on was first tested by Dr. Karl M. Dallenbach. He tested high-school graduates' memories of an episode they had seen which involved two strangers and in which they had no personal interest. They were tested four times: immediately after looking at the episode, again a week later, a week after that, and again six weeks after the original observation.

The details which they swore were gospel truth, but which were actually wrong, increased during the six weeks, as the chart shows.

The longer ago it happened, the more we need to check the facts before we trust our memories of them.

When brushing up old memories, better go back to the record and start afresh with an accurate account. If you don't, you're taking a real risk of imbedding "the facts" as you mis-remember them.

When describing a scene that was shown to a group, each person insisted as "the gospel truth" that he saw many things not in the scene. Retroactive falsification increased their misreports and made them more unreliable gossips as time elapsed. (From experiments by Dr. Karl M. Dallenbach)

5. *Why we mis-remember*

A memory seldom fades away uniformly, as a photograph does when left in the sunshine. Memories fade more in some parts of the picture than in others.

In addition, our memory pictures are retouched so that the original scene is almost always altered. The general outline may remain faithful, but we all have some personal motives for retouching the pictures so they look better to us when we fish them out of memory.

The individual is almost never aware of these motives for distorting his memories, or that he is twisting his memories out of shape. It is as if there were hidden imps who were playing practical jokes on our memory pictures without fear of being caught.

There are several well-established patterns by which the imps retouch, or distort, memories. The two scientists who pioneered in experiments to pin down some of the tricks of mis-remembering were Dr. William Stern, a German-born psychologist, and Sir Frederic C. Bartlett, psychologist at Cambridge University. Dr. Stern began the systematic study on mis-remembering because of its importance in evaluating legal testimony. Sir Frederic extended the study to additional reasons why we unwittingly distort our memories.

At the present time, several new experiments each year add to the knowledge of the hows and whys of mis-remembering. Here is a summary of some of the principal reasons which have been well confirmed and which can be grouped into two broad classes.

(a) We distort our memories to make the details more in line with the way we wish they were.

(b) We mis-recall so that the way we remember details seems more reasonable, or more as we would expect them to have been if our recollection gave us a complete picture, which it seldom does.

A close-up look at those two groups of reasons will be useful for pointing out ways to make our memories more trustworthy as we brush them up.

6. Distorting to support hopes and beliefs

Mis-remembering to make details more in harmony with the way each wished they were occurred with Mr. and Mrs. Otto R. He preferred to remember the meeting place as Washington Street, because that would be the shady side. She preferred to remember it as the State Street side of the store, because of the interesting window displays there.

Winifred Davis would have preferred a brooch that was a valuable piece of jewelry, rather than a cheap decorative trinket. So it grew in value in memory to support her hopes.

Remembering our successes rather than our failures is in the same class.

It is not surprising that prejudices and biases exert a great influence in the unconscious distorting of memories. We unwittingly pick and choose so that we remember details in a form that agrees with our beliefs, and forget what is not in harmony with them. More facts in favor of women as executives are remembered by women than by men.

And so it goes, day in and day out. Memories are retouched so they will be on the side of our hopes, beliefs, and prejudices. The net result is that how we remember many things tells more about our hopes and aspirations than it does about the thing itself.

7. Twisting facts to complete the picture

Mis-remembering so that it seems to make better sense, or so the details fit together, or so the picture seems complete or "comes out right," was evident with the Cambridge scientists.

Most of them reported that the chairman thanked the principal speaker. The chairman usually did that, but at this meeting he had not. The scientists "remembered" that he had, because it seemed in accord with what was expected at such occasions and fitted logically into their memories.

The distortion and addition of details is marked when experiences are ambiguous, or when they are incomplete and leave us with unfinished business.

A large share of everyday experiences occur so rapidly, or unexpectedly, that we get only a blurred, ambiguous impression. Accidents illustrate this. The conflicting "true accounts" that eye-witnesses relate show how remembering is modified to produce recalls which seem to hang together logically.

Hazy or poorly understood first impressions are good grist for distortion in the memory mill.

Reading, or speeches, are often in the ambiguous class. They are likely to be mis-recalled with more than usual inaccuracy because of the strong proclivity for the imps to organize our memories so we remember things as we think they should have been to make sense.

Names, of things as well as of people, are likely to be recalled incorrectly. This may be partly due to the nature of names; they are arbitrary and ambiguous labels. It is usually easier to remember the characteristics of people than their names. Their characteristics make more sense to us. So it is easier to recall a man as a tall, helpful salesman, while his name remains "Mr. Whoosis."

One of our most fundamental mental activities, many modern psychologists emphasize, is this tendency to alter memories and perceptions so that things seem complete and workable and practical to us.

Thus people often say "It had to be the way I remember" when they are grossly mis-remembering. This illusory feeling of clearness may be due to the way the imps have changed details, or added some, to make better sense to the person. In the distorted form in which he recalls it, he can understand it and it seems clear—it is clear, but as misleading as sleight-of-hand.

This leads us to a short but important chapter on what to do about mis-remembering.

CHAPTER 14

*Seven ways to make your memories
more trustworthy*

Do we have to put up with all that mis-remembering?

Much of it can be eliminated. Just *how* much depends upon the person. Cutting down mis-remembering takes more self-discipline than some people care to exert. But here for you to use, if you can discipline yourself to use them, are some precautions that seem worth taking.

1. Overmemorize early in the game. This is the surest safeguard against mis-remembering. Those who quit memorizing as soon as they have something barely memorized leave the widest openings for mis-remembering to fill the gaps which will be there by tomorrow.

There is plenty of time for overmemorizing. Refresh while on the bus, in the bath, barbershop, beauty parlor, in conversation, when dressing, while eating, while waiting, etc.

The problem is not finding the time, but of forming the habit of using odd moments for brushing up.

2. Keep tabs on accuracy. Check back to the record early and often. Eliminate errors before you convince yourself they are gospel truth.

3. Make written records to guide you. Play safe at the start; get the important details on paper, don't try to carry them entirely in your head.

Write a note (on a file card, for instance) immediately, not an hour later, when it will likely already be misremembered.

Dr. Paul Ehrlich, who won a Nobel Prize for his discoveries in medicine, made his notes at once on whatever surface was handy—his starched cuffs or shirt front, the wall, the door.

Write the date on these fresh memos of facts, new words, anything you should remember correctly. Carry each memo with you for a week, shuffling through the pack during odd times, and brush up each item numerous times during that week.

Some of the memos will be worth filing away for use to confirm—or straighten out—your memories in the future.

4. Check the record before reaching important decisions. Or, before making statements which could lead to arguments.

5. Get acquainted with your prejudices and biases. Understand what your hopes and aspirations are, as well as you can. After that soul-searching, keep those imps from tampering with your memories, as well as you can.

Challenge what you recall by asking yourself: "Is that the way it was, or could it be that I wish it had been that way?" "Was I to meet my wife where she preferred, or where I preferred?"

6. *Do some critical thinking whenever* mis-remembering is a possibility, as it appears to be about half the times. Become acquainted with common fallacies in thinking. Dr. Edward M. Glaser tried this with high-school students, and found that a few weeks' training produced considerable improvement in their critical thinking. Several books listed in the back of this book will be useful for this.

Critical thinking may lead you not to believe many things that others report as clear memories. But don't waste time trying to convince them how they have mis-remembered. It is a full-time job to keep your own remembering straightened out.

7. *Understand it from the start.* If it is ambiguous to you, the imps will have an easy job distorting it to make it appear clear. When it is not clearly understood after a few moments' critical thinking about it, you are likely to be beyond your depth and might better forget it completely.

If you haven't the time, or self-discipline, to take those seven precautions, better keep your fingers crossed whenever you say, "This is the way I remember it."

We have already noted that mis-remembering is helped along by the fact that we incline to remember mainly the high spots, so we mis-remember to fill in the gaps. In the next chapter we will take up some ways to prevent the gaps in the first place.

CHAPTER 15

Some remedies for half-remembering

1. WATCH ALL FOUR LINKS IN THE MEMORY CHAIN
2. STRENGTHEN THE SHOESTRING LINK
3. HOW TO WARM-UP RECALLING
4. KEEP CALM, COLLECTED, AND CONFIDENT

1. Watch all four links in the memory chain

We use the term *half-remembering* because of the many gaps in our memory of anything. Half-remembering is a kindly way to state it. In fact, we remember much less than half. We seldom realize how often we half-remember, as we are calling it, unless we keep count.

Franklin J., a beginner salesman in the appliance department, had a sales trainer who kept count on Franklin's half-remembering during the first hour of work one morning. These are some of the misses that were observed by the trainer.

Just before the store opened Franklin said, "There was something I wanted to ask you, but I can't think of it just now." Why did he say that?

Shortly after that he was hunting for his order book, which he (half-) remembered putting somewhere but couldn't recall where.

As the first customer entered the store, he whispered to another salesman, "We sold him a de luxe model yesterday—remind me of his name quickly."

While making his first demonstration of the day, the prospect asked how many watts of electricity it used. "I (half-) remember reading that in the manual," Franklin replied, "and will look it up if you really want to know."

When this prospect left without buying, Franklin said, "Come back and we'll make a deal before you finally decide, Mr. O'Brien." The prospect's name was Bryan.

His next customer asked the price of an automatic timing accessory he might want to have specially ordered. Franklin (half-) remembered that it was made in Ohio, but couldn't recall the price and guessed at a figure that was below cost.

Don't conclude that Franklin was a nitwit. We're all in the same boat with him—and a rather leaky boat it is at most times. Our memories are loaded with thousands of things we can only partly recall.

Why do we half-remember so many things? Probably because we assume that if we once register something, we will be able to recall it when we want to use it.

But registering, or memorizing, is only one link in the chain of remembering. We have to give attention to three other links to have an efficient memory which will pass the practical test of bringing back what we want when we want it.

Psychologists today look upon remembering as a series of distinct processes, which can be pictured as four links in a chain. These processes take place, one after the other, about like this:

REGISTERING——→RETAINING——→RECALLING——→RECOGNIZING

Each of those links has to be strong enough to hold the complete memory together if it is to be of full use to us.

Sad to report, efficiency almost always drops sharply and our memories fizzle out from one link to the next. Thus we register many more experiences than we retain as durable traces. In turn we retain more traces than we can recall. And, to top it, nearly half the time we cannot recognize whether what we recall is correct or not. This final link sometimes seems to be made of rubber which stretches things the way we wish they were.

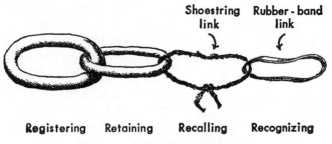

Diagram of the Chain of Memory

2. Strengthen the shoestring link

The two preceding chapters have dealt with that rubber-band link.

This deals primarily with the link ahead of that—the recall link. For most practical purposes, the recall link is the weakest. It holds the typical memory chain together about as well as a frayed shoestring would, as the diagram shows.

Recalling doesn't have to be the weakest link, but it usually is. This is understandable, because it is the Little Orphan Annie that we neglect. Consider Franklin J's half-remembering, for instance. He had had practically no practice in re-calling the half-remembered items. Practice in recalling them would have mended the shoestring link.

Usually the shoestring link becomes more frayed as time goes on. In one test of remembering meanings, it took 1.5 seconds to recall the meaning right after memorizing, or registering. The next day it took 2.4 seconds. A week after it took twice as long as at first.

Stewart M., who had just been elected president of his Junior Chamber of Commerce, had an embarrassing experi-ence which highlights the need for making the recall link stronger. The morning after the election he was working on some marketing plans when a reporter telephoned to get a list of the club's new directors.

Stewart had to think hard before he could recall the names. That afternoon he suddenly thought of another name he had omitted (thanks to the Ballard effect), but it was too late then to get it into the newspaper with the others.

What caused his shoestring link to fray so soon after the election?

Stewart had registered the names the night before, but had not practiced recall of them. There had been several blank periods in the meantime when he could have recalled them to himself, and stalled off the half-remembering. But being human, he did not practice recall of them until the reporter called, and by that time they were already elusive.

3. How to warm up recalling

When the telephone rang, Stewart was preoccupied with his marketing plan. To answer the reporter's question, he first had to switch his thinking from marketing to the club. That took a long time, it seemed, because the reporter had interrupted a task which Stewart wanted to finish. It was difficult to get that unfinished business off his mind, as Dr. Zeigarnik could have warned him.

And after switching gears to the club election, it took additional time to warm up his recall on the changed topic.

It takes time to warm up recall, even for memories that are well ingrained. It may take several minutes after switching gears. It is a mistake to give up trying before you are really warmed-up.

And in nine cases out of ten, it is a mistake to try to warm up by thinking specifically about the elusive item over and over again. If you keep pressing your memory for the missing item, you will likely get an assortment of mis-recalls (from the shoestring), some of which you will falsely recognize as correct (from the rubber-band link).

Keep at the recalling, but in a different fashion:

> Warm up recall with some concentrated thinking to refresh your mind on the situation in which what you want to recall happened.

Stewart *revived his memories of the original situation* by recalling the room in which the election had been held. He recalled what faces he could, where the people sat, the sounds of their voices. The details were recalled slowly at first, then with more speed as he revived the original situation in his thinking.

The details he revived also came steadily closer to the missing names for which he was rummaging. The detail that finally revealed the names (except one) was his recalling of the blackboard on which the votes had been tallied.

When you see someone you recognize, but cannot recall his name, use that method and revive the original situation. Don't bat your brains out trying to get the name directly.

And don't become panicky or embarrassed, for reasons we shall learn soon.

Simply recall what details you can of the original situation where you met Mr. Elusive Name. Who were some others present? What did they talk about? Why was he there? How was he dressed? What were his business connections? Where did he live? Such details as you recall in answering those questions will not only help revive the half-remembered name, they will also give you something to talk about while you are stalling for his name to come to you.

As you recall more details of the original situation, they will begin to cluster around his name. Then with a "click" the name is suddenly recalled.

Whatever it may be that eludes your recall, don't tug at the shoestring link. Strengthen it instead, by refreshing your memories on the original situation so the traces in the nervous system will be reactivated more adequately.

This coaxing, we might call it, is successful even for finding lost articles which have been absent-mindedly mislaid. But before we look at such applications in the next chapter we should learn why we need to keep an even keel when recall fails.

4. Keep calm, collected, and confident

When Julian Hawthorne sought admission to Harvard to study engineering, the timid youth was interviewed by an overbearing professor. The professor frightened the wits out of the would-be-freshman, who became so uneasy he could not recall his name. "Do you come to Harvard," the man bellowed at him, "to be taught your own name!"

When Clarence B. Randall went to the same college, nearly a half century later, he hoped to win distinction on the debating team. Peewee, as the 100-pounder was nick-named, memorized a five-minute speech for the tryouts. He had it letter-perfect in his room. But the night of the tryout he "went blank" after two minutes and could not remember even the topic he was talking about. He ran home and cried himself to sleep over his failure.

The coach, an old judge, saw through that failure. The next morning he hunted up Randall and promised to make a debater out of him if he would keep calm and composed in front of an audience. Randall did become a star debater, later rose to be chairman of the Inland Steel Company, and was for years an effective public spokesman for business leaders.

Many experiments have proven that emotions have a powerful effect upon remembering. They can affect the efficiency of registering, but the worst effects are usually upon recalling.

Emotionally tinged attitudes which lower recall efficiency, sometimes to zero, are:

anxiety	hatred
apprehension	feeling ill-at-ease
confusion	inferiority feelings
depression	injured pride
displeasure	lack of confidence
embarrassment	stage fright
frustration	shame
grief	

Keep those emotions out of your system when it is difficult to recall anything. Keep them out by pausing to compose yourself. Take it slowly, on an even keel, and you will be less likely to blow up.

Help yourself keep composed by recalling what you can about the original situation. That will give you something to

MEMORIZED BETTER WHEN THEY FELT CONFIDENT

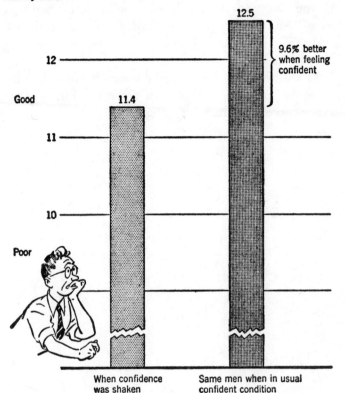

Memory score:

12.5

9.6% better when feeling confident

12

Good 11.4

11

10

Poor

When confidence was shaken

Same men when in usual confident condition

Memorized Better When They Felt Confident. Memorizing long numbers similar to telephone numbers was tested in 16 men. Later in the test their confidence was shaken by telling them there was something peculiar about their memory. Many other tests confirm these results which show how feeling confident helps use one's abilities. This experiment with numbers was by Dr. and Mrs. Stanley Moldawsky.

137

think about rather than your failure to get the elusive item at once. And it will also help coax it back to recall.

If you want to be absolutely confident of getting the elusive item, have it on a file card which you can turn to quickly. File cards and source books have no shoestring or rubber-band links.

Let's see next how these methods are developed to locate articles we have mislaid, and to resurrect other memories that are more than half forgotten.

CHAPTER 16

What to do when it is difficult to recall

1. The technique of posture-actions-and-mood

Special techniques are often needed to recall (a) what was registered poorly to begin with, (b) what we have had no practice recalling, and (c) unpleasant things we would rather not recall.

It helps revive the original situation in such cases if you can *go back to the location where it happened.* Students, for instance, recall more when they take examinations in the rooms where they studied for them.

Constance W., a private secretary, applied this principle when she had difficulty transcribing a sentence from her shorthand notes. She took her notebook into the office and sat on the chair where she had taken the dictation. Still she could not decipher the sentence.

Then, without leaving the chair, she leaned forward as she

had when making the original notes. She began to move her writing hand as if she were taking down the preceding paragraph—warming up to the puzzling sentence. As soon as her hand came to the troublesome notes, she recalled the correct meaning in a flash.

Her experience illustrates the helpfulness of doing a little more than merely thinking back about the original situation. It is the technique of reinstating the posture-actions-and-mood of the original situation.

The revived postures and movements are unusually useful aids for recalling. So-called muscle memories are especially durable. And there is almost always—some psychologists claim always—some muscle memory tied in with all other memories.

Revive the muscle memory by getting into the original posture and action, and presto! it arouses some deep-seated traces which give clues to the missing item.

Talking to oneself—for which we have had good words to say before—is a common method for reviving the muscle memories for names and technical terms. You have the vague feeling that Mr. Elusive Name is Irish. So you repeat Irish names until the right one rings a bell—but better verify it to be sure you do not falsely recognize it as correct, especially if you have pressed yourself to recall it.

2. *How the lost diary was found*

Prudence W.'s story illustrates the way some of our unexpected recalls come from an accidental revival of the original postures-actions-and-moods. She had imprudently mislaid her very personal and romantic diary, and prodded herself for days trying to think where she might have put it.

One day during a lull in her tormented search, she hurried to answer the telephone. The instant her hand touched the telephone a picture flashed into her head showing where she had put the missing diary.

Spooky? Not at all. It is a classic instance, reported by

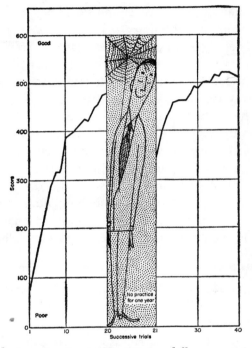

Muscle Learning Lasts. How motor skill was acquired in following a rotating disk with a hand pointer. The first 20 trials of one minute each are shown in the curve on the left. After a year of no further practice, the same 47 people tried the same skill, with results shown in the curve on the right. The learning of only 20 minutes' practice helped out a year later. (Courtesy Dr. Hugh M. Bell, Chico State College)

Dr. Joseph Jastrow, which illustrates the memory-reviving value of getting back into the original postures-actions-and-moods.

The day she lost the diary, Prudence had been lazily reading it when the telephone's ring cut short this romantic occupation. In her haste to answer the telephone, she made the blunder of slipping the diary behind the chair cushion instead of keeping it in her hand. (Always keep things in your hand until they are put in their regular places.)

When she hung up the telephone on that original day, she walked away on an errand, forgetful about her diary. Her action of hiding it had registered scarcely at all.

Now, on the Day of Discovery another telephone ring interrupted her when she was in the same chair, lazily reading a romantic novel. This was a close duplicate of the Day of Losing when she confusedly pushed the diary under the cushion. The ring of the telephone completed the situation accidentally, the nerve traces were aroused in a flash, and she pounced on the found diary with a squeal of delight.

3. *How the mislaid car keys were located*

Alton J., manager of a factory in a medium-sized city, had an experience which shows how these recalling techniques can be used intentionally. Late one forenoon he drove down town on several errands. He stopped at the bank, at the attorney's to sign some papers, then attended his luncheon club.

When he returned to the parking lot, his car keys were missing. Irritated because he was due at the plant for an appointment, he swore at himself as he fumbled in his pockets, on the front seat, and on the floor for the keys. The parking attendant did not have the keys, either.

Alton had an impulse to call the car dealer, but instead

took a determined breath, relaxed, and returned to the car. He would "use science" and find the keys by reconstructing the posture-actions-and-mood.

He climbed into the driver's seat and imagined he had just pulled into the parking space. When he went through the motions of taking the keys out, he realized in a flash that he had kept them jingling in his hand instead of putting them in his right hip pocket as was his usual habit. (Put things in their regular place!)

Then he recalled the errands he had in mind when he came downtown, and started to retrace his steps, imagining he had the keys jingling in his hand. He did not stare at the sidewalk looking for the keys, but tried to be occupied with thoughts that were similar to those he had had several hours before when he mislaid the keys.

As he rounded the corner to the bank it came back to him that in the original situation he had run into a friend at this point. He had stopped to visit with him about the industrial bowling schedule. He saw himself leaning against the mailbox as he chatted.

Then, almost without thinking, he quickened his steps to the mailbox and picked up the car keys which he had left on top of it.

Despite its high batting average, this method of reinstating the original situation does not always get results. The most common reason for failure is trying too hard to recall, which may be about like trying to catch a fish by the tail.

We should give our thoughts considerable slack when using this technique. Impatient people, who want to get through with the recalling in a hurry, defeat themselves. This is one instance where it pays to let one's thoughts have their own way. All we need to do intentionally is to reproduce the beginning of the situation, then let the traces revive themselves.

Whenever anything is elusive but worth recalling, give Nature a chance by reinstating the posture, movements, and mood which prevailed when it was registered.

And bear in mind to remain calm and collected.

4. The prime-and-wait technique

This technique is especially useful when the original situation happened so long ago that you would have to guess how to reinstate it.

Prime-and-wait simply means:

(a) Prime by thinking hard about it for a brief time, "to start the wheels turning."

(b) Then wait, letting the thoughts revive the traces in their own fashion.

This technique seldom brings the recall after the first priming. The first clues it brings to mind will likely be false, but nevertheless will have some bearing on the correct answer. So you have to prime yourself again on the clues that come out. The final—and correct—answer may pop out during one of the waiting phases when you are thinking about something else.

It was thus that Gilberta Y. found her lost engagement ring. Her first priming brought up thoughts of her vacation in a Connecticut summer camp. But she had the ring after the vacation, so that was a false lead.

Priming herself next on the summer vacation and letting her thoughts roam as they would, she thought of the washbowl of her room at camp. Then her thoughts shifted of themselves to the washroom where she worked.

A couple days later she picked up the threads during an idle moment. She primed herself with intentional thinking about the ring, then shifted to the washroom in her office. Scenes, as if in dreams, of public washrooms passed through her mind.

"Aha!" She flipped open her handbag and took out a small plastic box in which she carried a sliver of soap to use in public washrooms. The lost ring was stuck to the bottom of the soap.

When this technique is used to recall names, false leads are usually the first to come. But they are usually headed in the right direction, and should be followed by more priming-and-waiting.

For example, we have all had the experience of trying to remember a name. After one priming, we might say, "His name begins with 'G.'" The next false lead might be the name "Gault." Ten minutes later, while we are thinking about something else, the name "Vaulk" suddenly occurs—and that is the correct name.

We should not feel frustrated or discouraged by false leads. They seem to be necessary steps toward reinstating the correct pattern in the nerve traces. But it is important to make certain that what we recognize as the correct recall is, in truth, correct.

5. Five points in using this technique

The prime-and-wait technique is based on the fact that a large share of the 10,000 thoughts we have during a day seem to "just occur." Although they pop into mind unexpectedly, they have nevertheless been incubated by some internal activities which scientists do not well understand at present. But it is agreed that these thoughts are not as random as they may seem to an outsider. There's some reason why one kind of thought follows another.

The aim of the priming is to direct these internal activities to the topic about which we are concerned. To give them a mental set, so to speak. Or to motivate the spontaneous train of thoughts.

The aim of the waiting is to let the apparently spontaneous thoughts untangle the reluctant memory which they are now motivated to resurrect.

This technique usually requires several tries. We may have to prime ourselves a few times during one day. Or we may allow a day or two to lapse between primings, as Gilberta Y. did.

But we have to keep on the trail and not give up too soon. This does not mean we should spend all the time thinking about it. Quite the contrary. Waiting—patiently and collectedly—is essential.

During this wait we go on with our work as usual. But the internal activities set in motion by the priming continue on their own without our being aware of what is going on inside—a variation of the Ballard effect.

This internal activity takes place best when we do not interfere with it. So don't rack your brain by thinking directly about what you want to recall after you have done the priming.

A passive, abstract, or "blank" state is helpful to keep the incubation going. The triumphant "Aha!" is likely to come during a passive state. Symphony concerts, daydreaming, the bathtub, a walk, a monotonous ride, even church services have been good locations for this flash of recall.

There is also considerable evidence than an effective time to prime is when we climb into bed. That is when our thoughts usually begin to drift under their own power. When started in the desired direction at bedtime, the correct recall often appears "spontaneously" the following morning.

Here is a summary of how to use the prime-and-wait method, which is one of the most successful for recalling what was only dimly registered, or what has not been brushed up for so long that it has been largely erased by the avalanche of later experiences:

First: Prime, by thoughts that start reviving some of the traces involved.

Second: Go as passive as possible for a few moments right after priming.

Third: Then slowly resume your usual activities, preferably routines that do not require much thought.

Fourth: At some rest pause, or odd moment, prime yourself on it again, but passively.

Fifth: Continue going through those four steps at odd times until, probably in some abstracted moment, the recall suddenly comes to you.

Sixth: Then check the recall to be certain it is correct.

In household terms, put the right starting thought in the pan, then let it simmer on the back burner, stirring it gently from time to time.

Now we come to General Rule IV, which deals with the highest and most practical use of remembering, the storing away of meanings which we can use as the workhorse for thinking.

RULE IV

Keep your thoughts on the meanings of what you intentionally store away for binding time and as a workhorse for thinking

---

CHAPTER 17

Search actively for meanings

1. ONE WAY PADEREWSKI IMPROVED HIS REMEMBERING
2. MEANINGS MAKE MEMORIES MORE AIRTIGHT
3. MEANINGS SHOULD BE THE CHIEF AIM IN REMEMBERING
4. SEARCH ACTIVELY TO GET A STORE OF MEANINGS
5. THE MENTAL SET FOR SEARCHING FOR MEANINGS

1. One way Paderewski improved his remembering

Ignace Paderewski, the lonely, lisping boy who became the foremost pianist of his day, confessed that as a school-boy he could not remember music. He could play anything, and could improvise or compose, but he could not memorize music.

With poetry it was different. It was nothing for him to memorize three or four pages. Chess, too—he could play three games at once, from memory, with the chess boards and the competing adult players out of sight in another room. Why couldn't this lanky schoolboy who had been playing the piano since he was three memorize the music?

Something happened when he was fifteen, and he began to remember music as easily as he had played it. He credited this sudden zooming of his memory for music to a new teacher.

This teacher opened his eyes, for the first time, to the musical meaning in a selection. Suddenly music became more to him than pleasing sounds it was fun to produce. He began to catch on to the inner meaning of each selection.

Before tackling a new selection, the boy and his teacher looked it over first to analyze its musical structure. They discussed the effects the composer had in view, the mood of the selection, why independent melodies had been added as an accompaniment to the main melody.

As the teen-ager began to look for meaning in what he played, his playing became more expressive, more sincere, more promising for the brilliant future he was to carve for himself. And, of most significance to us in this book, his musical memory became as nimble as his long fingers which could caress or torment the keyboard.

2. Meanings make memories more airtight

His experience illustrates how greatly the efficiency of remembering is improved when we look for the meaning, or get some sense, from what we want to remember.

Remembering the names of people we have just met is difficult largely because the name has no meaning for us at first. The name might as well be so many nonsense syllables, and has to be registered by the bulldozing or endless repeating of rote memorizing. After we get to know the person better, his name brings many meaningful associations to mind and it is easy to recall the correct name at will.

We get all these advantages when we concentrate on meanings while registering something in memory:

It is usually memorized much more quickly.
It is almost always remembered much longer.

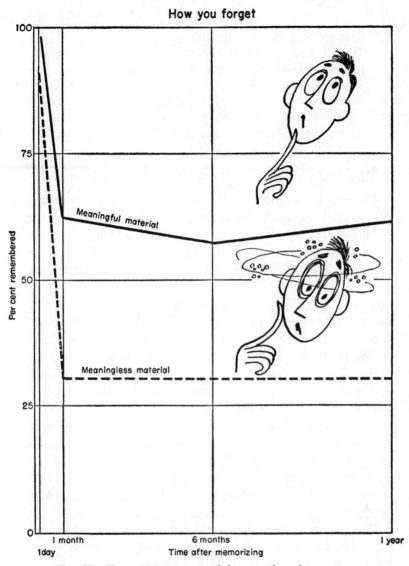

How You Forget. Memories stick longer when the meaning of the memorized item is clear. Strive to understand and to make the other person understand clearly. (Adapted from R. A. Davis and C. C. Moore)

It is not forgotten as rapidly.

There is more gain from reminiscence (the Ballard effect).

It is much less likely to be erased by later impressions (less retroactive inhibition).

Your chances of applying it to other situations are greater— you can make it work for you.

It supplies you with materials that are essential for problem-solving and adaptive thinking.

3. Meanings should be the chief aim in remembering

Charles F. Kettering, the scientist and inventor, was plagued by unusually weak eyes, which made it difficult for him to read. As he was working his way through college he did not read many of the lessons himself. Instead, he would lie on his bed while his roommate read the lessons aloud.

That was really good luck, Kettering claimed later. Since he couldn't read to himself, he was forced to concentrate on the meanings as he listened to his roommate. He couldn't review the lesson; he had to refresh the meanings in his head.

Supplying the materials for thinking—getting the meanings —is undoubtedly one of the most valuable uses of remembering.

It has been said that you can tell the difference between a boy and a man by what they remember. The boys remember details by rote, especially concrete details. They do not do much picking and choosing in what they remember; useful and useless memories are jumbled together, higgledy-piggledy.

But the men search for the details that make sense, and organize their memories around meanings, often abstract meanings, which the boys do not grasp.

Workers often remember as the boys do. Although they may have lots of know-how for their jobs, they may have scant know-*why* because they do not grasp meanings to remember from their work experiences. Until they begin to glean and to remember meanings, they will likely flounder whenever something comes along for which there is no ready-made answer they can call from their memories of tangible details.

Many star salesmen have become snarled up, for instance, when they were promoted to sales manager. They remembered products, talking points, prices, and credit policies well enough. But they had not extracted meanings which were needed to get to the heart of the broader problems they had to look ahead to as managers.

When a man is said to be "beyond his depth" it often means he has not remembered meanings which help him make better decisions to solve unusual situations that come up.

Some differences in aims between younger, or less successful, and the leaders in business bring this point home. A person who is starting in business tends to emphasize enthusiasm, remembering names and faces, and the other minor details of the day which have only momentary usefulness.

But those who get to the top generally report that it is more useful to remember the ideas (meanings) of longer-range business usefulness. Then they can get to the heart of problems and plan better for the future. They trust secretaries, or assistants, to tip them off on names and faces, while they search their own memories for meanings which can give them foresight and sound judgment for guiding the business.

The salary levels in a firm are closely in step with the amount of meaningful thinking the jobs require. The lowest pay goes to the jobs where workers merely go through the motions. The higher pay goes to the jobs where notions have to be understood, remembered, and used.

4. Search actively to get a store of meanings

How does one go about laying in a supply of meanings?

The three-pound, grayish-colored problem-solver within the human head does its most valuable work only when it is supplied with meanings. It circulates and retains these in significant patterns throughout its estimated 10 billion neurones.

The factory ships this amazing problem-solver without any meanings built in. All the meanings are optional equipment which have to be furnished by the owner himself. Teachers, parents, bosses, and books may give him some aid in supplying his problem-solver with meanings. But it is primarily a do-it-yourself job.

It is to be emphasized that the brain does not generate meanings spontaneously. If not supplied with meanings it generates hot air. The owner has to load the brain cells with information which makes sense and which can be organized and retained by the information-hungry neurone patterns.

We have to start from scratch by laying in memories which will make later experiences meaningful. It is not until around the age of three or four that we begin to catch on to meanings, and to remember them so they can be used by the problem-solver.

Before then we remember many details, but we do not connect or integrate them so they make workable sense. Thus most children think all men are "Daddy" for a few months after learning the word—to the embarrassment of the bachelor neighbor when he is called "Daddy." The first time they see snow many children call it "milk." A few months later they begin to get the meaning that "Daddy" means one certain man, and that whiteness is shared by many things other than snow and milk.

From such small beginnings in forming concepts, powerful

meanings are—or can be—slowly built up. They do not appear in full bloom, but are gathered together piecemeal in what can be considered four essential steps:

First: A person filters out meaningful impressions from his day-to-day experiences for special contemplation.

Second: He searches his experiences for what makes them work, or for the essence, or common element, or general ideas (concepts) hidden in them.

Third: Then, after he has gleaned some understanding, he gives these meanings top priority when registering later experiences in memory.

Fourth: He adds to, clarifies, and extends those meanings as he filters and searches and stores later experiences which bear on the meaning.

Meanings thus "grow on us." We get numerous flickers, or partial understandings, which we add to in the course of time. Gradually we catch the general drift—especially if we are searching for it, as Kettering did.

We have to take a crack at understanding it before we remember it. So long as we don't understand it clearly, we should keep going back to it, pondering over it, so that it can grow on us until we can view it in a clear, flickerless light.

A typical worker as he clears up some of the flickers in the meaning he gets of "costs" can be used as an illustration. The teen-ager who is beginning work can grasp the meaning of direct costs easily enough. But it usually takes some time for indirect costs to dawn on him. He may have to mature— and ponder—a few more years before he comprehends that the water cooler is a part of the costs. He may have a few flickers about fringe benefits being costs, but he may not include these in his understanding of costs because his comprehension of the meaning of profits is muddy, so he concludes that the fringes come from profits and are not a part of the costs.

5. *The mental set for searching for meanings*

We get meanings better when we are self-propelled to search actively for them—when we are motivated to clear up the flickers.

A few people do that so consistently that it seems "just natural" for them. Others need to cultivate an attitude, or mental set, or habits, to prod them to react fully to significant experiences and thus transform half-formed notions into soundly based insights.

Many executives post the brief motto THINK on their walls, but confess they don't know whether or not it has made them think. This is plausible, because the one-word motto merely reminds them to think, and does not give them directions about how to start. They might be more certain of results if they added some directions, like this:

THINK
Search actively for meanings by asking yourself *thought-provoking questions*

Until the mental set of searching actively for significant meanings becomes a habit, it may be helpful to keep something like that how-to before your eyes as a reminder to look for and register more meanings. And to react fully by looking for the sense.

Understand it first, and it is almost automatically remembered and in its most valuable form.

What kind of questions are thought-provoking? The following chapter will give you some answers.

CHAPTER 18

How to put on your thinking cap

1. ASK YOURSELF THE RIGHT QUESTIONS
2. ASK YOURSELF FILTERING QUESTIONS
3. "HOW DOES IT WORK?"
   "HOW COULD IT BE USED?"
   "WHAT ELSE COULD WE DO WITH IT?"
4. "WHAT DO I REMEMBER THAT BEARS ON THIS?"
5. "IN WHAT WAYS DOES THIS HAVE A DIFFERENT MEANING?"
6. "HOW DOES THIS JIBE WITH WHAT I ALREADY REMEMBER?"
7. "HOW COULD I EXPLAIN THIS TO SOMEONE ELSE?"

1. Ask yourself the right questions

Within a couple minutes a four-year-old asked: "Why don't all dogs have short tails?" "Do all dogs bark?" "Why do dogs dig?" "Are there some dogs as big as elephants?" "Why do dogs bite?"

Such questions seem to be Nature's way to help children get more meanings from the world they live in. Their incessant, and at times embarrassing, questions round out their conceptions and lead them to broader-gauge ideas that can do better work than a hatful of narrow-gauge ideas.

With adults, too, questions are a mainstay for any one who wants to get at the meaning of things. But there is this difference: the adult should ask himself the questions, because the purpose is to prod himself into searching for the mean-

159

ing, or for a fuller meaning if he already has a few flickers.

Merely figuring out a pertinent question usually milks some meaning. And the more you understand something, the easier it is to think of more questions which will bring out the cream of the meaning.

Any old question will not do the job. "How many," "Where," "Who" questions have little thought-provoking value. They are purely and simply recall questions. They do not prod you to pause-and-think about meanings, which should be the aim of the questions. If the question can be answered by a word or fact from memory, it is not reasonable to expect it to add to your supply of meanings.

Here are some generally accepted qualities to strive for in the questions you ask yourself, if they are to lead you to search for meanings.

2. Ask yourself filtering questions

"What of it?" "What significance does it have?"

Those are good filtering questions for starters. They are especially useful for separating what is not worth remembering from what should be given top priority. They keep memory from becoming a catchall for irrelevant details.

The man who conscientiously remembered all the drinks of ale that had been given him was not applying this type of question. Neither are those people who memorize the early election returns.

It is being applied when one underlines the phrases which are most significant in his serious reading. More about this in the next chapter.

"How many did we sell last week?" is simply a recall question that anyone could answer without a flicker of meaning.

"Why didn't we sell as many as the week before?" is different. It will tease you into searching for some meanings (or alibis?).

"Why" questions head you to think about cause and effect. The causes you think up will likely be suppositions which need to be checked, either by logic or test—but either way your supply of meanings is extended.

3. "How does it work?"
"How could it be used?"
"What else could we do with it?"

These questions provoke more detailed thinking about causes and effects. They are usually applied to gadgets or machines, but can also be used to get a better working understanding of such intangibles as investment plans, or the processes of remembering.

They also lead one to search out new meanings for old, familiar things. They can bring out inventive, or creative, meanings to store in memory for future reference or application.

4. "What do I remember that bears on this?"

This prods you to look for similarities in meaning, and to classify and organize meanings. Some will belong together, and can be tied into a package, or general principle, that sums up the essence or common feature that is imbedded in several experiences.

Thus larger, and more abstract, meanings, begin to replace, or combine, bits and pieces of meaning as more things are linked together.

Executive training programs which shift the trainee from one department to another are applying this principle. This shifting is not done to make the trainee skilled in the various operations. Rather it is done with the hope that he will have a better working grasp of the business as a whole as he searches a variety of departmental experiences for their interrelated meanings. The trainees who get the motions but not the notions will likely end up at routine work in some department.

5. "In what ways does this have a different meaning?"

At the same time you are asking the preceding question, you should also be asking this one. Not everything which at first thought seems to belong together does belong together.

Words which are assumed to have the same meaning provide examples of the need for this question for clearing up muddle-headed thinking. We commonly assume that many pairs of words have the same meaning, such as: growth—development, genuine—authentic, component—constituent, constant—continual, nomenclature—terminology.

As a matter of record, however, only one pair of words in the English language are regarded as exact synonyms: gorse —furze. All other so-called synonyms have somewhat similar meanings, but without exception have slightly different exact meanings.

Another example of the need to look for differences in meanings comes from the fact that a large share of our words have more than one meaning. Before you conclude that you remember the meaning of the commonly used word "through," better recall as many meanings of it as you can. It has at least thirteen! We need to spot the meaning in which a term is used if we are to keep our thinking on the right track.

By searching for ways in which seemingly similar things don't belong together, you can bring out different shades of meaning that need to be remembered so your thinking can be more accurate.

6. *"How does this jibe with what I already remember?"*

This question may lead you to filter out some of your new experiences, and to put fresh props under old ones.

Suppose you had a chance to buy at a bargain an ancient Greek coin that was dated 500 B.C. You do not need to be an expert at coins of that period to tell whether it is genuine. And you can tell without looking at the coin, if you apply that question.

When new experiences, or meanings, conflict with those we remember, it may be because our memories are inaccurate. You can't always be as sure as you probably were about that coin that your memory has stored up the meaning correctly. This part of the search may send you back to the record—those file cards, or a source book—to straighten out some of the errors which are inevitable in recalling.

7. *"How could I explain this to someone else?"*

This is regarded as one of the best tests of how well one has caught the drift of the meaning. Job trainers often use this test—they ask the trainee to give the job instructions in his own words.

"I have the idea in my head, but can't find the words to say it" may mean you have discovered a wonderful new idea for which there are as yet no words. But it almost always is a confession that you have only a muddy notion which you need to clear up before it will mean anything to you, or to anyone else.

A useful technique for letting the mud settle is to put the memory into words. Talk it over, or explain it to someone else. Or try to explain it in a brief memo so that it will make sense to someone else.

There will be considerable floundering on your first few tries to express a new meaning you are developing. You will likely talk or write in circles until, at last, the meaning clicks and you can exclaim, "Aha! Now I understand it clearly enough to use it!"

Don't get so busy, or so overconfident, that you neglect to ask yourself some of those questions as you are taking in new experiences. Pause-and-search among your thoughts for their answers so your problem-solver will have a useful supply of significant (filtered) materials to work with.

Next we will see how we can get more meanings to remember out of what we read.

CHAPTER 19

How to remember more meaning from what you read

1. IT REQUIRES A SPECIAL MENTAL SET
2. WHEN TO USE THE MENTAL SET FOR SERIOUS READING
3. WARM UP BY REFRESHING YOUR MEMORY
4. PREVIEWING HELPS WARM-UP
5. DO A THREE-PART PREVIEW OF A NONFICTION BOOK
6. QUESTIONS TO KEEP YOU ON THE TRAIL OF THE MEANINGS
7. WHEN TO UNDERLINE AND MAKE MARGINAL NOTES

1. It requires a special mental set

"I stopped reading as soon as I finished high school," we sometimes hear people confess. They usually add, as an excuse, "Because I seldom got anything out of it." That explanation is really an admission that the person has not learned to read for meanings.

It was much different with Thomas A. Edison, who had only three months of formal schooling. Somehow he taught himself to read for meanings. "When I want to discover something," he said, "I begin by reading everything that has been done along that line in the past."

He had one of the most complete scientific libraries of his time. It was claimed that he could walk directly to any of the 10,000 volumes without having to wonder where it was on the shelves.

Reading is one of the principal ways to supply the raw materials which are needed to support the problem-solver.

That is one reason for the training which many firms are giving supervisory and managerial employees in rapid reading. Brief as these courses are, they often double the speed of reading.

Those increases in reading speed do not mean that the eye muscles were trained to move more rapidly than before. The speed comes from learning to grasp ideas or meanings. Instead of reading word by word as in the past, they learn to read a meaningful phrase at a glance.

Speedy readers almost invariably read for meanings. Consequently they not only get more out of what they read, but also remember it better.

Sad to say, our usual reading habits do not help us read rapidly, or get much meaning out of what we do read. This is because of the inclination to read everything as though it were recreational reading—done to kill time. And done mostly with the eyes (and lips), and with scarcely any active searching for meanings.

The mental set used for recreational reading is scarcely suited for getting much meaning, as the following columns make clear.

RECREATIONAL reading *"The everyday way"* ↓	*SERIOUS reading* *"The trained way"* ↓
Body relaxed, slumped, lethargic	Body poised, alerted, reactive
Pick-and-choose something interesting	Filter out trivial; concentrate on significant
Pleasure-seeking attitude	Want-to-know attitude
Look for entertaining episodes	Search for meanings
Pause to daydream	Pause to ponder meanings
Let thoughts roam as they wish	Pull thoughts back to topic

RECREATIONAL reading "The everyday way" ↓	SERIOUS reading "The trained way" ↓
Look at pictures for enjoyment	Study charts for what they show
Skip new words	Use dictionary
Hurry straight through	Back up to clarify meanings
Quit if bored, or reading becomes difficult	Keep at it to finish job (Zeigarnik)
Take sides with characters or viewpoints	Weigh information impartially, looking for whole truth
Remembering is incidental	Intend to remember it a long time
Doodle	Write notes; underline Ask thought-provoking questions of self

The way to get your money's worth out of a book or magazine is to follow the column on the right.

2. When to use the mental set for serious reading

When you want to get meanings from reading you have to switch on the mental set, or frame of mind, described on the right. This will aim you point-blank at getting and holding the sense.

Switch on that mental set whenever you read:

business letters	occasional magazine articles
contracts	once-in-a-while news stories
directions	reports
instructions	some advertising
insurance policies	specifications
legal documents	technical journals
memos	trade journals
nonfiction books	what else?

As with all techniques we learn, we will not master this mental set instantly. It requires continued self-direction at the outset to hold to the mental set for meaningful reading. More self-direction than usual may be needed, because of a life-time habit of using the recreational set.

So you will find yourself lapsing back to daydreaming in the middle of a paragraph, or skipping new words, or not looking for the key thoughts. These lapses may cause you some anxiety, which is a good thing if it prods you to pull yourself back into line. The anxiety about brief backsliding is harmful only if it discourages you to give up, as some do after high school.

It takes not only practice, but also motivation, before you can safely switch on the mental set for serious reading and let it run itself.

3. Warm up by refreshing your memory

It will be easier to hold on to the mental set for serious reading if you do some warming-up just before reading.

One effective technique is to take a few moments to recall some of the things you already know about the topic. Do this before settling down to read. This not only gets you into the swing, but also nails up some familiar hooks on which you can hang the facts and meanings you will gather from the reading.

Edward Gibbon, who had been too sickly as a child to get much formal education, used that method. By it he helped educate himself to become the chief authority on the 2,000 years of *The Decline and Fall of the Roman Empire*. He un-earthed the sources for his history in rare Greek and Latin manuscripts; he read thousands of them, for their meanings.

Before reading a faded record, he would actively search his memory for what he could recall on the topic. After this warming-up, what he read "snapped naturally into place," and the meanings were firmly anchored within his memory.

Give your head a head start by refreshing your thoughts before tackling the reading. To do this, you need to have a fair idea of what the reading is about. So you will need to preview.

4. Previewing helps warm-up

Get an idea of what it is about, how it goes, and how it ends, before plowing into it. Thumb through or scan the chapter, article, or report before reading it thoroughly. Notice the main headings, and what the pictures, charts, diagrams, and tables portray.

Such a preview gives several advantages in addition to putting more heat into the warm-up. You get some flickers about the sense before doing the close reading. You get a general view of the whole which will make the parts hold together in memory. You will also spot the parts which will be of most relevance for you, and which you will want to read more thoroughly.

A similar preview is useful before reading a lengthy business letter or document. See the thing as a whole before taking it up part by part.

Previewing is easy, almost unavoidable, when the writer has provided an outline at the beginning, and meaningful subheadings throughout. Tests have shown that a preview outline at the beginning is more effective than a summary at the end when presenting subject matter. (Get the meaning of that sentence straight. In *reading* subject matter, it is still highly efficient to pause at the end and summarize in your thoughts—recite to yourself—the gist of what you have just read.)

In the case of letters and memos, you can write a preview in a sentence at the beginning, telling what it is about. This is required in most military correspondence.

The thought-directing sentence, outline, and subheadings should be worded so they will start the reader thinking in directions which will help him grasp and hold the meaning. The purpose is not to arouse curiosity or to entertain, but to sharpen the reader's outlook for the meanings of what follows.

What do you do, as a reader, when there are no outlines and subheads to sharpen your outlook for meanings?

Then you will have to sample the opening sentences of individual paragraphs. Usually, but not always, the first sentence gives an idea of what the paragraph is about. You can generally preview by skimming the opening sentences, but it takes more digging and more time than where there are subheadings which are not ambiguous.

In those few instances where first sentences do not reveal the points the paragraphs deal with, you will have a difficult and perhaps meaningless job reading it. Some writers present material in a coy manner, as if it were a detective mystery; they conceal what they are driving at. A few others ramble, mixing relevant and irrelevant material which would be more than a Solomon could outline. This is the case with too many business letters and reports, and with a large amount of conversation.

When you get hold of coy or rambling reading which has ambiguous first sentences and tricky subheadings, you have to wrack your brains trying to unravel the meaning. You might be further ahead if you substituted another book or article which covers the topic with a well-organized outline and subheadings which you can grasp at a glance.

5. Do a three-part preview of a nonfiction book

When starting a nonfiction book do a preliminary three-part preview to size up the book as well as to tune up your thinking:

1. Note the date it was published, or revised. Is it up-to-date? If not, it may still be worth reading to clear up your thinking with an historical perspective on the topic. But know from the start whether it is ancient or modern so your thinking will not be behind the times.
2. Look at the table of contents. Are the chapters organized into groups? Why are they grouped that way? Then read down the chapter titles to get a notion of the general drift of the book—and accept our condolences if the chapters have coy titles.
3. Then read the preface. Read between the lines to decide whether the book gives one person's unproven views, or whether it presents established facts upon which authorities agree. It may be worth reading in either case, but know what you are reading and guide your thinking accordingly.

This three-part preliminary may cool off rather than warm up your set for reading the book. It may lead you to decide that you want a more elementary or a more advanced book. It may not be what you thought it was from the beautiful cover. It may not be what you thought it was from the title; titles may be unintentionally misleading—*Unresting Cells* does not deal with prison life, or flashlight batteries, but is an authoritative book about the life processes in the cells of the body.

Perhaps a preliminary preview will cause you to question the soundness of the book. If the claims for the book seem extravagant, and you are not sure of the author's integrity, ask a professional librarian or some authority in the field about the author's qualifications.

If you are still warmed up after that three-part preliminary, and you probably will be, thumb through and scan the first chapter. Now you should be in a moderately warm state to read the chapter seriously and profitably.

But, unless you have had Edward Gibbon's long practice, you are not as warmed up as you can be. It will probably take fifteen minutes or so of diligent reading to complete the warm-up. From then on, until some form of fatigue overtakes you after sixty to ninety minutes of reading, your train of thought will be making maximum headway and loading on most meanings to circulate around inside your head.

6. Questions to keep you on the trail of the meanings

Now that you are mentally set and warmed up, make the most of these advantages by asking yourself suitable questions as your thoughts plow across the lines. There will be less fatigue, and your thoughts will plow most deeply, uncovering more meaning for you, if you

> Keep asking yourself thought-provoking questions
> And pause to answer each in your own words.

Every three to five minutes there should be a question which springs from what has just been read. By asking yourself these questions at short intervals you will be more certain of getting the meaning straight early in the game—fewer half-truths and vague notions to cause trouble later.

In addition, the frequent clarifying pauses give the meanings a better chance to jell securely—less erasing of the traces by retroactive inhibition.

Each question should be answered in your own words, or own thoughts.

If necessary, read back or consult a dictionary, to clear it up.

The questions should be about meanings, about significances. Not about bare facts, but questions which will tie together your memories of various meanings. Open-ended questions which cannot be answered by a single word or statistic. Such as those we met in the preceding chapter:

> "What is he driving at?"
> "How does it work?"
> "How could it be used?"
> "What else could be done with it?"
> "How does this differ from something similar to it?"
> "How does it jibe with what I already remember?"
> "What is most worth remembering from this?"

One purpose of such open-ended questions is to keep you in a questioning frame of mind—a "want-to-answer-something-that-counts" mental set.

After enough experience, and with adequate motivation, that problem-solving attitude can become a habit whenever you do serious reading. When that stage of self-development is achieved, you will no longer need actually to ask yourself the questions. But until you have the habit, play safe and actually ask and answer the questions.

"No man really becomes a fool," Charles P. Steinmetz, the wizard of electrical engineering, commented, "until he stops asking questions."

7. When to underline and make marginal notes

Underlining, or making check marks √, can be extremely helpful. Deciding what to mark, and what not to, makes you filter the sense and focus on the meaning more than you might do otherwise.

And the marks speed up reviewing, or hunting for an item later. It is easier to reply to a long letter and omit nothing, for instance, when you have previously checked √ the points in it which should be answered.

But underlining and check marks can lead you into blind alleys.

Don't underline or check the first time over unless you are fairly expert on the topic about which you are reading and have really clear meanings instead of flickers.

If you are not clearly familiar with the topic, the first time through read with a dictionary at your side, if necessary, and write the meanings on the margin of your reading. But no underlining yet. Any underlining or checking at this stage of your comprehension is likely to be on a blind-man's buff basis, and will trap you the next time you read through the material.

The second time through, however, take your pencil in hand and underline. On this trip search actively and rapidly for the key phrases (seldom single words) that are most significant for conveying the main sense. Then underline, or √, the essential high spots to blaze a meaningful trail through the jungle of words.

Marginal notes, or *diagrams,* can be safely made on the first reading. (If it is a borrowed book or journal, write them on file cards, but be sure to write down the page number and location to which each note applies.)

On the second reading you will likely change some of these marginal notes. That is a good sign of progress, of clarifying your ideas.

One of the principal uses of marginal notes is to nail down sudden bright ideas before they vanish. It may be an idea you get of a possible application, as twenty-year-old George Westinghouse got the idea for air brakes from reading about tunnel construction in an engineering journal. It may be an idea comes to you about something you want to look up, or try out, or call to the attention of an assistant—write it down immediately.

And write it down in enough detail that you will know what you had in mind when you read the note the next week.

When buying secondhand books you may have noticed that those with underlinings and marginal notes are priced the lowest. Resist the temptation to save a half dollar. The underlining has probably been done by someone before he was familiar with the topic—an expert seldom sells his books, even the out-of-date ones.

Amateurish underlining usually makes hash of the sense. The amateur asks himself pointless questions, if any, and underlines nonsense as well as a few flickers of sense.

Your own underlining, of course, will not be amateurish, because you are doing it the second time over.

Why bother about remembering? It is everybody's business. All the time.

It cuts a wide swath in our workaday lives. It is a universal biological function which enables living creatures to steer their actions and thoughts so they can cope successfully with life.

It affects the efficiency of our work.

It is the workhorse of mental activity, providing information and meaning for the brain to work with.

It is, unfortunately, almost always done at a low level of efficiency.

But its efficiency can be increased several-fold if we:

    I. Have a *mental set* to remember at the time
   II. *React actively* to experiences worth remembering
  III. *Refresh* and *straighten out* the memory of it at strategic times
  IV. *Search actively for meanings* which are time-binding and which give information that is worth circulating around the brain.

So here we are at the end of the book, and, we expect, you are already more efficient in your remembering.

Recommended readings

It is unfortunate that many popular publications dealing with memory are based on questionable assumptions. It has accordingly seemed desirable to provide the reader with lists of books which he can trust. These lists are not complete, of course, and are our selection of books we recommend as a starter.

Bookstores may not have these in stock, but can order any of them for you from the information given here. Large libraries will have most of these books. Smaller libraries can get copies for you on interlibrary loan from larger libraries.

Self-help books

Most of these can be read by a high-school graduate.

Barzun, Jacques, *The Modern Researcher*. New York: Harcourt, Brace and Company, Inc., 1957. Excellent material on making notes, on remembering what one reads, and getting the meaning. Don't let the title frighten you away, though the book is abstract in spots.

Bennett, Margaret E., *College and Life*. New York: McGraw-Hill Book Company, Inc., 1952. Intended to help college students, includes helps on choosing a vocation, life conduct, etc., as well as memory.

Brothers, Joyce, *10 Days to a Successful Memory*. Englewood Cliffs, N.J.: Prentice-Hall, Inc., 1957. Although titled like a patent medicine, this is a peppy, encouraging, and sound book by a professional psychologist.

Cole, Luella, *Students' Guide to Efficient Study*. New York: Rinehart & Company, Inc., 1946. A thin book, widely used, and giving excellent helps on making notes, underlining, etc.

Ham, Arthur D., *Doctor in the Making*. Philadelphia: J. B. Lippincott Company, 1943. A general guide for the medical student; explains why there are better ways to memorize anatomy than by using code rhymes.

Linton, Calvin D., *How to Write Reports*. New York: Harper & Brothers, 1954.

Mantell, Murry I., *Orientation in Engineering*. Englewood Cliffs, N.J.: Prentice-Hall, Inc., 1955. A thin book of suggestions for engineering students.

Morgan, Clifford T., and James Deese, *How to Study*. New York: McGraw-Hill Book Company, Inc., 1957. A thin, paperback manual widely used by college students.

Nichols, Ralph G., *Are You Listening?* New York: McGraw-Hill Book Company, Inc., 1957. Helps for remembering and getting the meaning out of speeches, conferences, interviews.

Preston, Ralph C., *How to Study*. Chicago: Science Research Associates, 1956. A thin book, aimed at high-school students.

Robinson, Francis P., *Effective Study*. New York: Harper & Brothers, 1946. Emphasizes efficient methods of reading for meaning and remembering.

Souther, James W., *Technical Report Writing*. New York: John Wiley & Sons, Inc., 1957. A small book.

Tuttle, Robert E., *Writing Useful Reports*. New York: Appleton-Century-Crofts, Inc., 1956. A sizable book covering a wide range of writing and note making.

On remembering in general

These are more difficult reading than the books in the preceding list, and although there is much practical information in them it is not given emphasis.

Barnards, Harold W., *The Psychology of Learning and Teaching*. New York: McGraw-Hill Book Company, Inc., 1954. A textbook for would-be teachers. Fairly easy reading; practical; good material on how to develop interest.

Bartlett, Frederic C., *Remembering*. New York: The Macmillan Company, 1932. His first study of distortions in remembering.

Deese, James, *The Psychology of Learning*. New York: McGraw-Hill Book Company, Inc., 1958. A discussion of facts and theories of remembering, presented for college classes.

Guthrie, Edwin R., *The Psychology of Learning*. New York: Harper & Brothers, 1952. A general survey of the facts, and some theories; many examples from daily life.

Hilgard, Ernest R., *Theories of Learning*. New York: Appleton-Century-Crofts, Inc., 1956. For the advanced student; much material on animal learning.

Hunter, Ian, *Memory: Facts and Fallacies*. Baltimore: Penguin Books, 1958. A pocket-size paperback for the general reader. Explains how to use some of the old-time "systems."

Miller, James G., *Unconsciousness*. New York: John Wiley & Sons, Inc., 1950. The most complete survey of work on "unconscious memories."

Rapaport, David, *Emotions and Memory*. New York: International Universities Press, 1950. A reprint of his 1942 book on selective factors which make remembering untrustworthy.

Rotter, Julian B., *Social Learning and Clinical Psychology*. New York: Prentice-Hall, Inc., 1954. Deals technically with the role of remembering in maladjustment.

Thorndike, Edward L., *The Psychology of Wants, Interests, and Attitudes*. New York: Appleton-Century-Crofts, Inc., 1935. Some of his now classical experiments reported in a way that is easy to read.

Thurstone, Louis L., *Primary Mental Abilities*. Psychometric Monograph No. 1, 1938. Technical account of his factor analysis studies which indicate that each person has several kinds of memories which are fairly independent of each other.

On reactivity and brain processes

Unless you have some background in biological sciences, you will need a medical dictionary at your elbow when you read these.

Cameron, D. Ewen, *Remembering*. New York: Nervous and Mental Disease Monograph No. 72, 1947. Reactivity problems in old age and in nervous conditions.

Cohn, Robert, *Electroencephalography*. New York: McGraw-Hill Book Company, Inc., 1949. A standard manual dealing with the electrical waves from the brain.

Eccles, John C., *Neurophysiological Basis of Mind*. Oxford: Clarendon Press, 1953. Lectures this famous Australian physiologist gave at Oxford University.

Laslett, Peter (Ed.), *The Physical Basis of Mind*. Oxford: Basil Blackwell, Pub., 1952. Accounts by several authorities in physiology and neurology.

On meaning

Barnard, Chester I., *The Functions of the Executive*. Cambridge, Mass.: Harvard University Press, 1947. A standard somewhat philosophical—yet practical—discussion of the meanings which mean most for executive work.

Bartlett, Frederic C., *Thinking*. New York: Basic Books, 1958. A high-level supplement to his book *Remembering*.

Chase, Stuart, *Guides to Straight Thinking*. New York: Harper & Brothers, 1956. Discusses thirteen common fallacies and their correction.

Hayakawa, Samuel I., *Language in Action*. New York: Harcourt, Brace and Company, Inc., 1946. A little book which gives a stimulating account of how general semantics deals with meanings.

Katona, George, *Organizing and Memorizing*. New York: Columbia University Press, 1940. Research on the importance of meaning in remembering.

Keyes, Kenneth S., *How to Develop Your Thinking Ability*. New York: McGraw-Hill Book Company, Inc., 1950. An easily read guide to applying general semantics to get meanings straight.

Ogden, Charles K., *The Meaning of Meaning*. New York: Harcourt, Brace and Company, Inc., 1927. A philosophical discussion, by the inventor of basic English.

Piaget, J., *The Child's Conception of the World*. New York: Harcourt, Brace and Company, Inc., 1929. Reports of his studies on how children form meanings.

Ruby, Lionel, *The Art of Making Sense*. Philadelphia: J. B. Lippincott Company, 1954. His popular radio programs converted into a book dealing with logic in everyday life.

Vinacke, W. Edgar, *The Psychology of Thinking*. New York: McGraw-Hill Book Company, Inc., 1952. A college textbook.

Index

ABOUT THE AUTHORS

Dr. Donald A. Laird is the author of more than a dozen books on self-improvement subjects and, in recent years, on selling and business techniques. After receiving his Ph.D. degree from the State University of Iowa, Dr. Laird taught psychology at Colgate University and also served as director of the Colgate Psychological Research Laboratory. In *Techniques for Efficient Remembering* Dr. and Mrs. Laird present practical methods for remembering, based on sound principles of psychology. Eleanor C. Laird, a graduate of Pembroke College, is co-author of *Techniques for Efficient Remembering, Sound Ways to Sound Sleep, The Techniques of Delegating, Sizing Up People,* and several other books.